KARTIN

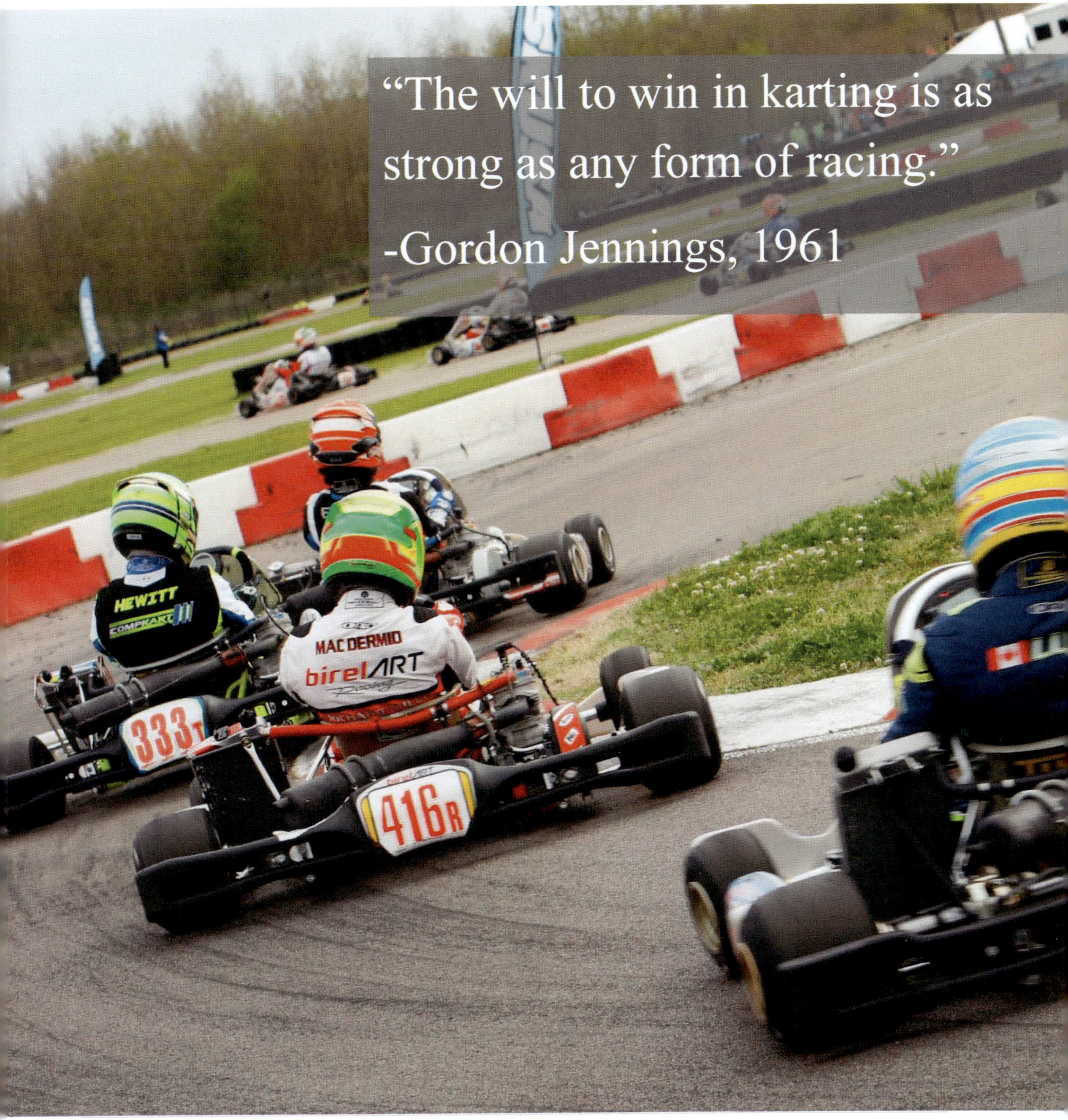
"The will to win in karting is as strong as any form of racing."
-Gordon Jennings, 1961
HEWITT
COMPKART
MAC DERMID
birelART
333T
416R

Table Of Contents

Forward	**4**
Introduction	**5**
Back to Basics: Karting History	**7**
The Go Kart: A Fundamental Overview	**10**
The Main Types of Kart Racing	**14**
Sprint Kart Racing	15
Oval Track Kart Racing	17
Endurance "Laydown" Kart Racing	19
Karting Age Classes	**21**
Kid Kart (5-8)	23
Junior 1 (8-12)	25
Junior 2 (12-16)	27
Senior (16-30)	29
Masters (30+)	30
Karting Engines	**32**
50cc Engines	36
60-80cc Engines	38
100cc Engines	40
125cc Engines	42
200+cc: 4-Cycle Engines	45
Kart Racing Series	**49**
Local Karting	50
Regional Karting	51
National Karting	53
International Karting	54
Karting Officials	55

Safety Equipment	**60**
Helmet	63
Suit	65
Shoes	67
Gloves	68
Rib Vest, Chest Protector	69
Neck Protector	71
Kart Maintenance: Tools and Equipment	**74**
General Tools and Equipment	76
Karting Retailers	82
Transporting a Kart	83
"What Now?" Taking Your First Steps into Karting	**85**
Visiting Your Local Kart Track	86
Visiting a Karting Event	88
Test Driving a Kart	90
Indoor Karting	92
Guidelines for Purchasing Your First Go Kart	94
Conclusion	**98**
About the Author	**99**
Acknowledgments	**100**

Forward- A Note from the Author

My foray into karting began with a picture of a go kart in a magazine. That first feeling of curiosity at the strange looking machine lead my family to get into the sport. If you are reading this, then you likely have experienced the same impulse I once had. Like me, the thought of driving, competing, and dare I say, *winning*…that has captivated you at some level.

I began racing go karts when I was 11 years old. While the journey from the back of the pack to the front was not easy, life lessons about the importance of preparation, competition, and challenging one-self continue to serve me each and every day, whether at the kart track or not. Lately, I have been able to view karting from new and humbling perspectives. Time spent as an official and as a driver coach has made me realize the true breadth of experiences this sport can bring to participants. Now, I want to share the sport of karting with you.

It is my hope that "Karting 101" will serve as one of many resources you may find in your initial research on the sport of karting. I can't tell you how many times I have been approached by someone at the track asking: "hey, what are these things?!" Other times, I encounter someone that wants to get involved, but doesn't even know where to begin. **"Karting 101" was created to educate interested members of the general public about the sport of karting.**

It should be noted that this document was not created without the help of more people than one can list. Also, it should be noted that the karting community has already taken dramatic steps to bring the sport in front of a wider audience. Websites like Ekartingnews.com, Comet Kart Sales' own "Karting 101," KartPulse.com, and books like Memo Gidley's "Secrets of Speed" are irreplaceable. My friends and fellow racers at The Colorado Karting Tour, The Colorado Karter, and Kart Pulse have all served as sources of inspiration, critique, and advice.

As karters, I believe that it is our responsibility to educate and inform others about the sport we love. I sincerely hope that this document will be of benefit to you, and help you understand what karting is all about, and what it can be for you.

--Eric Gunderson

Chief Instructor, Apex Predator Driver Development

Introduction

As I wrote "Karting 101," the one section that I continued to edit and tweak was this one - the introduction. After all, I reasoned, *this is my one chance.* I have to grab your attention with what I believe is the essence of karting. After all, what is karting really *all about*? Is karting about the performance and capability of the machine? Is it about motorsports competition at an accessible level? Or is karting simply a means to set and achieve increasingly challenging goals, and sharing your success and failure with a dedicated group of friends and competitors? I realized through this questioning that I couldn't make this introduction enthralling for everyone. I can't sell karting. To most, karting will sell itself.

Whether an experienced racing driver or someone that is new to performance driving, a go kart offers the most direct and thrilling driving experience one can experience in a vehicle with 4 wheels. With a seating position a mere inch from the racing surface, the sense of speed and performance one experiences in a kart is sure to bring a smile to even the most hardened racer. Through the corners, karts simply outperform any other vehicle. With some practice, driving a kart at speed becomes as much an act of will as it does hitting your turn in points and apexes—the steering in a kart is so direct that when properly set up the kart will often seem to drive itself. For many that have only driven a fully suspended racing or road car, the limits of grip in a kart are often astounding. It is not at all uncommon for drivers to experience lateral and longitudinal forces in excess of 3 G's in the corners in high-performance karting machines.

Some begin karting at a young age, with dreams of becoming the next world champion. Others get into the sport because they like to tinker, to perfect, and to consider the many peculiarities of a mechanical system. Perhaps you are still unsure why karting attracts you! If the past is any indication, you are not alone in this trepidation: Karting has historically attracted people from a wide background of occupations, income levels, and ambitions. Whether you idolized Ayrton Senna, Jeff Gordon, or Michael Schumacher on TV, one thing is true of over 90% of the world's current professional racecar drivers: they began to learn to drive and race in go karts. Many of these racers return to karts regularly to practice their fundamental skills, and stay involved in the sport that helped them fall in love with racing in the first place.

The sport of competitive go kart racing is considered by many to be the most affordable, fundamental, and exciting branch of motorsports available worldwide. Performance go karts are light weight and agile vehicles. Karts come in a variety of sizes and speeds, and accommodate racers of all ages, starting as young as 5 years old. With a back-to-basics approach to vehicle dynamics, karts race wheel-to-wheel at racetracks across the globe. They bring the excitement, speed, and challenge of motorsports competition to thousands of racers each year.

Kart races are held at varying competition levels, which means that a new driver can learn, improve, and continually find new challenges by competing against other drivers, visiting different tracks, and compete in a variety of racing series. Karting is both a singular and team sport; on the track, it is up to you to drive, enjoy yourself, and be safe. In the pits, it takes a community to learn from each other, and to make sure that each day at the track is a success.

Karting is at its essence a family-oriented sport. In many cases, a family may begin their karting adventure with their son or daughter as competitors. Soon, however, many parents may decide to race as well. Whether at the track for a competitive race event, practicing, or simply working on the kart with friends, karting teaches racers of all ages life lessons that extend far beyond karting. In particular, karting families will continue to stay involved because of the lessons in sportsmanship, attention to detail, and mechanical know how they and their family gain from the sport.

In the following sections a 40,000-foot overview of various aspects of the sport of karting is presented in a (I hope) fairly objective manner. Each section touches on a key component of the sport. "Karting 101" begins with a look at karting history, then transitions into a discussion about the basic components one can find on every kart. Next, the three main types of kart racing (Sprint, Oval, and Endurance/Laydown) are outlined. In addition, an overview of the varying levels of competition one can find in karting are discussed. One of the most important sections for all racer to read is the safety gear section, which touches on all the key gear a karter needs to compete and drive a kart safely. Various engine packages are outlined in general detail, illustrating how karting takes a progressive approach to incrementally matching ever-increasing performance of the engine package with the age and experience of the driver. Towards the end, a brief discussion regarding some of the must-have tools for working on a go kart are outlined, as well as a brief discussion about the methods to obtain parts for your kart, and transport them to and from the racetrack. Lastly, one of the most useful sections for new karters gives some tips about how to learn more about karting within your local area. For some, a section may be obvious, or not entirely relevant. In this case, I suggest and urge you to peruse the table of contents, find sections which are relevant to you, and read those in detail.

No matter your budget, background, or mechanical aptitude, karting is a sport that can be enjoyed fully and safely by a wide array of people. Together, it is those people that make the sport truly special. The support, camaraderie, and thought that most karters have for their competitors and for the integrity of the sport is inspiring and also humbling. "Karting 101" provided me an opportunity to take a step back, reconsider what the sport means to me, and inform others. Now, after over 100 pages, countless re-writes, and a myriad of ideas, I have concluded what karting is all about: It's about the people.

Art Ingels and Lou Borelli with an early prototype of their go kart, which would become known as the Caretta West-Bend (mid 1950s). Early karts utilized small engines designed to be used on chainsaws of the day. (PC: Radne)

Back to basics: Karting History

On a sweltering summer day in 1956, Art Ingels set down his bossing mallet and shot bag to take a quick smoke break. He had worked most of the day to perfect the shape of the front radiator shroud of his latest project—a midget racing car. It was just like several midgets he had already built for customers, who loved the performance and sleek lines the workers at Kurtis Kraft pulled from steel stock and sheets of aluminum. While he may not have realized it at the time, Mr. Ingels and his employer would become synonymous with Southern California car culture. In many ways, his latest side project, which sat in the corner of the shop on a work table amongst his usual clutter, would do the same for all of motorsports, not just midget racing.

Like so many men in So Cal, Ingels often contemplated fast cars, and the high banks of Ascot Raceway and Orange Show Speedway. Art often wished he had his own race car. He wanted to drive with speed and grace--just like Parnelli Jones or Mario Andretti. Ingel's gaze wandered over the midget car slowly taking shape before him. He noted the disparate elements present in

7 | Karting 101: An Overview of Competitive Kart Racing

this machine. While each was useless alone, they came together under his hands to make a machine that drew hundreds to the stands at makeshift stadiums across the country. A frame…an engine…4 tires…brakes…steering…a seat…it all seemed so simple.

It was simple. So simple, in fact, that Art's project-- his first 'go-cart'--was essentially a scaled-down version of the basic elements he saw in the race cars he worked on at his day job. A few days later, Art and his friend Lou Borelli would lift their creation off the table, and roll it out of the large rolling door at the front of the shop. As the evening sun began to lower over Glendale, California, a pull-start of the anemic McCullogh lawnmower engine they had attached to the steel frame signaled the beginning of something new. In that moment, the sport and industry of competitive kart racing was born.

From the very first public test of their kart Ingels and Borelli were inundated with orders for kits, and tips on how others could build their own kart. The first Caretta West-Bend kart quickly began to compete against other go karts. Over the next few months, more and more people flocked to the exhibition races that were held in parking lots around Pasadena, California. Within a few years of its invention, the go kart was spreading worldwide. Manufacturers, purpose-built tracks, and supporting companies began to sprout up to support the growing karting industry.

A historic kart sits at a contemporary event, awaiting its turn on track. By the mid 1970's, karts had evolved substantially, as this model demonstrates. Note the complex chassis geometry, wider rear racing slicks, and revised engine mounting location. (PC: CustardClub)

Today, karting continues to grow. Go karts and parts are shipped from manufacturers in Europe, The United States, South America, Asia, and Australia. Local, regional, and international events provide gathering places for racers to compete and celebrate karting. In the last 60 years, more drivers have begun their auto-racing careers in karts than in any other form of motorsport.

While karts continue to become faster, and the research into them more exotic, one thing has always remained very, very simple: Go karts are still little more than an engine, a frame, 4 tires, a seat, and a steering wheel. Go karts of today are the result of Art Ingel's initial design, and decades of refinement, experimentation, and revision.

Art Ingel's humble invention has gone world-wide. Local, regional, and international karting competitions are held every year, and attract kart racers and racecar drivers from all over the world. (PC: OnTrack Promotions)

While interesting, a short history lesson on karting is not the final word on the sport. After all, many things still need to be discussed. In particular, a deeper dive into those simple components Ingels brought together should be conducted. In the next section, a discussion about the basic components every go kart features will be undertaken. By the end of this section, hopefully you will have a greater understanding of some of the key pieces that are present in the construction of each and every go kart, no matter the specific chassis type or racing application.

Every modern racing go kart is the result of decades of development by major kart manufacturers. The engineered ability of a kart to 'hike' it's inside rear tire in a corner is the key to the astounding cornering ability most karts produce. Here, a kart demonstrates perfect wheel hike as it travels around a corner. (PC: OnTrack Promotions)

The Go Kart: A Fundamental Overview

What began as an amusing toy that brought a sense of motorsports to the masses has evolved into a true thoroughbred of performance. The term 'go kart' has become synonymous with quick and responsive performance among the motoring community. While the ultimate performance of each kart can vary, a properly set up kart can corner at high rates of speed with only a small turn of the steering wheel. As a result of the kart's chassis design, grippy racing slick tires, and an extremely low gross weight, drivers of karts regularly experience cornering forces of 2-3 g's, far beyond the capabilities of most other vehicles. The extremely low seating position in a kart also heightens the driver's sense of speed and the thrill of driving over most other racing vehicles.

As outlined previously, a go kart is typically composed of several key components: A chassis, rear axle, wheels, brakes, a seat, and of course, the steering wheel. Together, all these components must work together in a symbiotic fashion—that is, they must work together to deliver performance on the track. In this section of Karting 101, a brief explanation of each of these components will be performed. Because engine packages used in karting vary significantly based on factors such as geographical region, age of driver, and racing series, this particular component will be covered in its own section a little later on in "Karting 101".

A kart chassis (in blue) with associated componentry, with the seat absent. In this case, this chassis is intended for sprint kart competition. Note the steering, solid rear axle, brake location, central gas tank, and plastic bodywork. The two parallel rails on the right of the chassis are the typical location for mounting an engine. (PC: Comet Kart Sales)

The chassis is the backbone of any kart. Each chassis is composed of steel tubing sections, which, when welded together, form the main frame and structure of the kart. The bodywork, axle, engine, seat, pedals, wheels, and steering componentry all attach to the chassis. The arrangement of these sections, their thickness, and overall chassis geometry is critical to the on-track success and performance of every go kart. Manufacturers the world over spend countless hours researching and developing their chassis to give the best performance.

At the core of each go kart's ability to corner with such extreme force is the use of a solid rear axle. This axle is attached to the chassis by 2 or 3 bearings, which handle both the spinning and twisting forces that the axle will exert upon them. While this may appear old fashioned at first, a kart's unique ability to 'hike' or raise its inside rear tire as it begins to turn into a corner allows for karts to drive around corners with astonishing speed. Years of development have refined this ability in karts to the point that the rate at which this hiking happens can be varied, or 'tuned.' Expert karters know how to adjust their driving and chassis settings to make this behavior work in their advantage. Axles are available in various lengths, thicknesses, and styles.

Just as important to a kart's handling ability as the axle, the tires and wheels of most karts are designed to provide superior cornering performance. In most cases, a kart is equipped with racing 'slick' tires. The term 'slick' is in reference to the tires lack of tread, which allows for a much greater contact patch between the kart tire and the racing surface. Karting tires are designed to deflect and flex significantly as the kart corners, providing maximum contact and grip around the entire corner. The brand, size, and even compound of tires a particular kart may use varies significantly based upon the geographical region of competition, suppliers on hand, or type of racing. In certain conditions, special 'rain' tires with flutes that allow for the expulsion of water can be fitted if the track has significant water on its surface.

The kart seat has evolved over the years considerably. Note the flat bottom of this seat, which allows for a lower mounting position. The silver-sheen of this karting seat suggests that this seat features reinforced cross-weaving of the fiberglass, which ads durability and performance. Also, note the silver seat strut mounted to the rear of the seat, providing additional grip to the rear tires. (PC: KartSport NZ)

Another important component that is key for the performance of the kart and the comfort of the driver is the seat. Karting seats are designed to form around the body with adequate side support, to support the driver's torso, lower body, and back, and come in a variety of sizes to suit every driver and seat position. While many materials have been used to make karting seats over the year, the two primary materials for seats are fiberglass or carbon fiber. Unlike many other vehicles, a kart seat is designed to flex and deform subtly as a kart corners. Just like axles, the rate of deformation of a kart seat can be controlled by the seat material and mounting position.

The steering componentry of a go kart is relatively simple, and has been refined over time to provide the best steering performance while remaining as straightforward and light as possible. A steering shaft connects the steering wheel to two 'tie rods.' These tie rods are subsequently attached to components known as spindles, which attach the front wheels to the main chassis, and turn the wheels in a corner. While the alignment, geometry, and dimensions on these components can vary from kart to kart, this steering system is universal to all performance karts. As with most vehicles, the brakes on a kart are one of the components that are too often taken for granted, yet are extremely important. Karts typically use only one disc brake, but can be equipped with up to 3 (two front, one rear) depending on the performance requirements of the kart. On most karts, the brake caliper is found on the left side of the chassis and is mounted near the rear axle, which supports the steel or ceramic brake disc. Brakes on karts can vary in stopping power, design, and adjustability significantly, but all fundamentally do one thing: stop the kart.

Lastly, plastic components known as bodywork mount to the main chassis of the kart. These components are usually made out of a hardened plastic, and protect the driver and other competitors in wheel-to-wheel interactions, and provide a fuller, sleeker aerodynamic profile to most karts. These components are supported by strong steel brackets and bumpers to protect against more severe impacts. In 2008, the FIA, one of the leading sanctioning bodies for karting worldwide, implemented 'full' rear bumpers, which further increased protection for drivers and karts by widening the rear bumper dimensions to prevent karts from touching wheels inadvertently. While bodywork does serve many functions, racing karts are still considered open wheel vehicles, and accidents can still happen, albeit with decreasing occurrence.

Hopefully, this brief overview has given you a very basic understanding of the varied componentry that goes into each and every go kart. Together, these key ingredients are what make go karts truly performance machines. In the next section, a discussion about the different types of kart racing will be held. As you will see, while all karts are fundamentally constructed with the same key ingredients presented here, racers have, over time, found several variations of venue, kart style, and racing style that have led to the diverse world of karting present today.

Competitive kart racing comes in a variety of forms. As a result, karts are designed to suit different types of tracks, drivers, and engine packages. Making sense of it all can be daunting at first. In this photo, a group of sprint kart racers begin a race. (PC: On Track Promotions)

The Main Types of Kart Racing

The world of motorsports is diverse—the result of years and years of passionate members of the racing community finding ways to turn anything with wheels and an engine into something that can be competitively raced. While very different in fundamental ways, a super cross event and the 24 Hours of Le Mans are both motorsports events. In a similar way, the sport of karting has several forms of motorsports competition that a new racer can choose to get into.

While some regions of the world only host karting events sparingly, other areas have consistent karting events, hosted by local karting or regional karting organizations that utilize nationally and internationally recognized rule sets and safety procedures. In particular, greater Europe, the Americas, Australia, Asia-Pacific, and some island nations have regular kart racing events at a variety of levels of competition.

Depending on the geographical region a potential racer is located in, he or she may find that one form of karting is the most popular, and is therefore the most likely to catch their interest. In the name of thoroughness, the most common forms of kart racing found worldwide have been outlined in the following sections.

Sprint Kart Racing

Sprint kart racing provides some of the most compelling racing action a spectator or racer can experience in motorsports. In this photo, sprint kart racers navigate a series of corners during a race. (PC: On Track Promotions)

Over the last 30 years, the discipline of sprint-kart racing has continued to grow in popularity. While oval track karting and 'endurance/laydown' karting are also popular forms of racing in the United States, the majority of major karts produced worldwide are for sprint kart racing. If a kart track is near you, it is likely designed for sprint karts.

The term 'sprint-kart' comes from the fact that most sprint kart races typically last a shorter period of time than other forms of kart racing. Depending on the age of the drivers in a racing class, the level of competition, or venue, races are typically 10-15 laps in length, and take about 10-15 minutes to proceed from start to finish—a true 'sprint' timeframe for a racing event in motorsports. Sprint karting drivers often are very skilled at making many precise passing maneuvers in a short amount of time, as drivers must learn how to capitalize on each and every passing opportunity or chance to defend for position in such a short race.

A sprint-kart is designed to make both right and left turns, on tracks usually up to 1 mile in length. Often slightly lighter and more agile than their oval track or endurance racing counterparts, sprint karts achieve the highest levels of performance through the corners of any type of kart. With every minute input of the steering wheel, these karts tend to respond rapidly and precisely.

Sprint kart tracks are often smaller-scale versions of many famous racetracks across the world, with corners inspired from tracks like Road America, Laguna Seca, or Sebring. This of course means that sprint kart tracks are 'road course' type race tracks, with a variety of corner geometries, long and short straightaways, and considerable elevation change present in every track. These tracks can be very challenging to learn, and many karters enjoy the challenge and thrill of exploring new racetracks near our outside of their main region of competition. Sprint kart tracks can also be made from 'street courses,' temporary circuits set up near or in city centers to bring karting to those that may not get to see it otherwise, and to challenge karters with new types of tracks. One of the most famous street races, the Rock Island Grand Prix held in Illinois, draws over 20,000 spectators each and every year, with several hundred karters taking part.

Sprint kart races are typically held on racetracks that feature both left and right hand turns, with varying geometries that can make for a challenging circuit. Understanding how to plan and plot a course around these tracks, called a racing line, is extremely critical to success on race day. Here, Podium Karting in Centennial, Colorado, hosts a karting event. (PC: Mitch Bowers, Imagewerx.com)

16 | Karting 101: An Overview of Competitive Kart Racing

Oval Track Kart Racing

Oval track kart racers compete on a wide variety of racetracks. With varying surface composition, length, and even banking, track conditions can change more dramatically from lap to lap on an oval track than on a sprint track. Being on top of how the kart and venue will change throughout a race is critical. (PC: AZKA)

Like other forms of karting, oval track karting has been around for decades, and is extremely popular in certain regions of the United States and elsewhere. Like sprint kart racing, local, regional, and national events exist for oval track karters to test their skills against dedicated and skilled competitors.

An oval track kart race can be run on a variety of surfaces. Typically, oval tracks for karts use either dirt or asphalt for their track surface. These tracks vary in size significantly--from $1/10^{th}$ of a mile 'bull rings,' where bumper-to-bumper, close physical racing is common, all the way up to larger tracks ¼ mile in length or longer that are also used for larger machines like stock cars. At larger tracks, drafting and a smooth driving style are required to time passes, and to win races.

'Dirt' oval tracks can have a variety of surfaces used for racing: some use well-packed clay, some can be soft dirt, and some are even sandy surfaces. This creates for a wide variety of challenging driving conditions that racers must master in order to be a proficient and fast oval kart racer. Some tracks are flat with little banking in the corner, while others have very high banking that creates higher speeds over the same length of track. When compared to sprint kart racing, the length of the oval track races varies significantly based on the overall size of the race track. Because track conditions can change rapidly on oval tracks, racers have to focus considerably on how their kart's handling will change as the race progresses.

While not quite as popular or numerous as dirt tracks, asphalt oval tracks challenge racers with similarly diverse track conditions, and the fact that an oval track racer must always be at the very limit of his machine's capabilities to win races. As stated before, many asphalt oval track karting events are held at facilities that cater to other forms of racing vehicles as well, such as quarter midgets, stock cars, and open wheel racing.

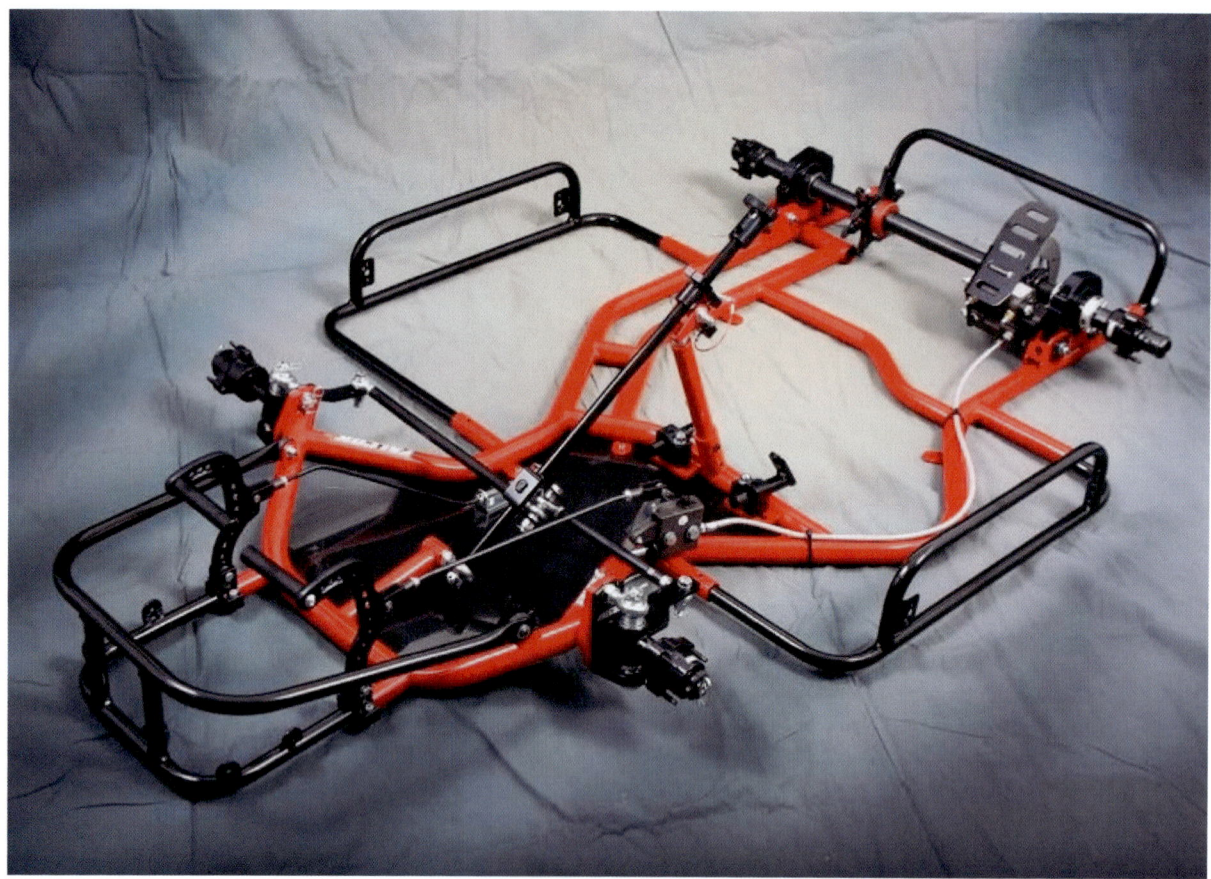

An oval track kart chassis, with seat, tires, and bodywork removed. Note the offset chassis structure (naturally to the left). In many ways, this chassis is exactly the same as a sprint kart chassis, but critical components like the driver's seat position, steering, and even bodywork are offset to cater to left turns.(PC: Southern Express Karting)

Oval track karts are typically made with the purpose of turning left as their first priority. This is evident almost straight away when one examines oval track karts. The chassis are typically off set, meaning that certain frame components are intentionally skewed to the left of the centerline of the chassis. The seat is also placed to the left of center, typically at a lower angle as well. Another notable difference is the use of 'full' bodywork, and different widths of tires on the left or right sides of the kart. While still very fast and agile vehicles, performance figures for an oval track kart depends largely on the type of track surface it is driven upon.

18 | Karting 101: An Overview of Competitive Kart Racing

Road Racing/Endurance Karting

At a glance, 'lay down' endurance or road racing karts tend to have a sleek appearance, like this beautiful example driven by Rick Fulks of Team RRR Racing. When compared to their sprint kart brethren, these karts feature a longer wheelbase (distance between front and rear wheels), and compete at larger, flowing race tracks usually used for racecar competition. (PC: Fade to Black Photography)

Road racing or 'endurance' kart racing events are known for featuring a wide array of chassis brands, designs, and engine packages. Endurance karting events can vary in length, largely dictated by the level of competition and venue at which the karts are competing.

While many road racing/endurance karting events allow for sprint karts to compete in separate classes at the same event, endurance-style karts are generally designed to best suit fast and flowing racing venues. Around kart tracks or race shops, the term 'laydown' is also common when referring to road racing or endurance karts, as some have the driver seated in such a way that it appears he is laying down in a position more reminiscent of a street luge than a kart, for aerodynamic purposes. Traditional endurance karts are typically longer in length than their sprint kart counterparts, and can be slightly narrower in overall width. In addition, many utilize bodywork that closely resembles that of oval track karts.

Together, these changes mean that endurance karts are more suited to being stable at higher speeds, and in broader, sweeping corners. These machines favor a driver with smooth inputs on the steering wheel and pedals, and perform well at the larger venues that they race at. Most endurance karting events take place on tracks that are also used for other forms of road racing, such as motorcycle or full-size car racing. Laguna Seca, Road America, and Daytona all host endurance karting events most years. While not as fast as many of the machines that may race at these circuits at other times, the low-to-the ground body position means that a driver's sense of speed is highly elevated, and the thrill of high-speed drafting and strategy is a big draw for many endurance kart racer and enthusiasts.

Another slight variation on road racing and endurance karts are so called 'super karts.' With large engines, tires, and often additional aerodynamic bodywork, these karts are capable of speeds at times in excess of 150 miles per hour. While not as common a sight at the track, they are hard to miss when they are there, as their pace through the corners and down the straightaways is dramatic. (PC: Kartlink.net)

Regardless of which form of kart racing you choose to get involved with, there are some important common practices that most forms of kart racing adhere to. In particular, the general manner in which drivers of different ages are divided by classes, how drivers work to gain experience in karting with drivers of a similar ability, and the progression of the costs associated with different levels of karting competition tends to be similar across karting's several forms (sprint karting, oval track karting, endurance racing).

In the next section, a brief explanation of many of the common karting classes available will be discussed. While the classes presented are particularly relevant to karting within the United States, almost all major forms of kart racing and regions utilize a similar methodology to separate kart racers based on age, experience, and resultant kart performance. It should be noted that this section is a general guideline, and the age divisions presented are not hard rules, but rather common practices for most karting series. **To learn more about which karting class may be right for you, consider reaching out to your local karting community, to learn about the common class structures put in place in your region.**

Like many sports, karting is separated into different age categories, known as karting classes. These classes allow drivers to race against others with a similar skillset and weight. (PC: OnTrack Promotions)

<u>Karting Age Classes</u>

Like many other sports, karting is a sport that has been designed to be accessible to competitors of all ages. As a result of the wide array of ages present at any karting event, kart racing is separated by age classes. Through the class structure system, karting series are able to give drivers an amount of performance that best suits their current age, ability, and budget.

Within karting, the two main methods used to categorize drivers into racing classes are the age of the driver, and their resultant cognitive ability. This is because a driver aged 5 years old cannot be expected to to handle the same amount of performance as a driver in his mid-30's. As a result, a driver at age 5 may start in the Kid Kart class, which races with scaled down, less powerful versions of their bigger brothers in the Shifter Kart class. As one would expect, the ultimate top speed of these two classes is very different, and this is by design: 40 mph for a Kid Kart, and over 110 mph for a shifter kart at many tracks.

Drivers of different ages can enter into karting through the class system, which allows for a progressive increase in the size of the kart, and resultant performance. Here, a kid kart (left) sits alongside a cadet kart powered by a Rotax MicroMax engine. (PC: Radne)

Drivers can begin racing go karts competitively as young as the age of 5, and many karters are still at the track competing well into their 70s. Karting classes help racers of all ages compete against other drivers with similar abilities, and help to ensure that racing events can be run smoothly and safely.

In this section, the focus will primarily be on the classes that are commonly found at every race series and track across the United States. While the names of the classes, the exact ages of the divisions, and the type of kart racing may change, almost all karting series utilize karting classes at events. It should be noted, however, that the precise age brackets and raw performance of karts present at any event or hosted by a particular series can vary significantly from one region of the world to another. While age and ability to process the performance of the kart are the most critical methods for separating drivers into classes, other factors that can vary include the engine package used, type of tire, and of course, the size of the kart.

In the following pages, a brief outline of the most common classes found at sprint kart racing events will be outlined. Over the years, each class has gone by many different names, largely reflective of the engine packages that are used or are in vogue at this particular moment. Each class will have a particular age range for the drivers that compete in the class, and each class also features some characteristics unique to the drivers and karts present within the class.

Kid Karts

Aspiring drivers can begin racing in the Kid Kart class at the young age of 5. This class is intended to teach young drivers the fundamentals of competing in racing events while at a safe and approachable top speed. Note the pedal extenders, padded seat, and Comer 50cc engine, which puts out approximately 2 horsepower. (PC: Chloe Chambers)

The youngest drivers can get involved in karting is at the age of 5. At this age, a driver will almost certainly be placed into the Kid Kart class. This category uses karts that are specifically designed at a size and weight that will allow for a young driver to experience his first racing machine safely. The chassis of these karts are approximately ½ scale when compared to a kart intended for adult use. As a result, most kid karts weigh approximately 100 pounds without the driver, and about 140-150 lbs with the driver and all safety gear.

In this class, most drivers begin to learn the very basics of racing. Most importantly, they learn how to participate in a kart race safely, and have fun! Because these karts do not travel at a high rate of speed, and because most drivers at this age do not drive the kart to its absolute performance limit, the wear and tear on these karts is minimal when compared to most karting classes.

For many young racers, Kid Karts are the first step into serious motorsport competition. Sometimes, this can mean learning to race in adverse track conditions. Here, a kid karter competes in wet track conditions. Note the grooved rain tires and plastic cover to keep water out of the air filter. (PC: PKT Axles)

Most modern kid kart chassis are designed with many options to adjust that ensures that the driver is very comfortable in the kart, with less focus placed on adjusting the go kart itself for performance. Traditionally, these karts usually utilize a small, 50cc 2-cycle engine. However, 4-cycle engines with comparable performance have become more common in recent years, and still allow drivers to learn the basics of racing at a slow speed with full safety gear.

To find out more about the Kid Kart class, it is a good idea to consult with local karting series to see what their specific age requirements are, and what some next steps may entail. In most racing series, drivers can progress on from the Kid Kart class at the age of 8. In some cases, drivers that have passed the age of 7 may be allowed to 'move up' to the next racing class, which is Junior 1.

Junior 1

The Junior 1 category is often one of the best classes to watch all race weekend long at any track. Drivers that enter this category learn very quickly how to race well with others, and how to improve their own driving and performance through adjusting the kart chassis and their driving line. (PC: On Track Promotions)

Once a driver progresses beyond the Kid Kart category, or turns age 7 or 8, he or she may enter the Junior 1 category. Unlike kid karts, this category can go by many different names. In addition, the size of kart chassis is considered to be the 'cadet' size, and so these classes can be called by some the 'cadet classes.' These karts are considerably faster than the kid kart class, but still not as fast as many karts intended for adult use.

As mentioned previously, Junior 1 classes utilize the 'cadet' size of chassis, which is approximately ¾ scale of a full size kart. Adjustable front end geometry, various seat options, hub material, and axle type all play major roles in the setup and performance of any cadet kart. While the top speed is dependent upon the engine package attached to the kart, cadet karts usually weigh 220-250 pounds with the driver and safety gear, and can achieve top speeds in excess of 70 mph.

Within this division, the name of the specific class you may find at the track will be primarily governed by the type of engine package used. For example, many Junior 1-aged racers currently compete in karts that utilize the Rotax Micro Max engine. Therefore, instead of Junior 1, their class is called Micro Max. Other names for classes for drivers of this age and experience level include Rookie Sportsman, KPV-1, and Mini Swift, which are all different engine packages that are affixed to kart chassis that are the same size and performance within the class.

Because of the popularity of the Junior 1 age class, sometimes karting series will have more than one Junior 1-level racing class on hand during a racing weekend. Primarily, the difference between these classes will be the engine package on the kart. (PC: On Track Promotions)

The term Junior 1 is still utilized by many racers and members of the karting community when they refer to these classes due to the long-time endurance of a cadet class that utilized the Comer K-80 engine, which was called Junior 1 by many racing series the world over. Initially implemented in karting in the late 80's, the Comer K-80 engine platform can still be seen at local karting events in competition.

Once in Junior 1, drivers will begin to experience *significantly* more heated competition. Due to more powerful engines, higher performance tires, and more chassis adjustment options available, a driver's ability to give feedback about the kart's performance, improve their driving, and refine their race craft (their strategy and ability to race and pass others) comes more to the forefront than in kid karts. Significant local, national, and international competitions are also available to drivers in Junior 1 classes.

While each region may vary their age classification slightly, most drivers will race in Junior 1 until the age of 12 or 13, beyond which they are considered ready to progress on to the Junior 2 classes.

Junior 2

Designed for racers aged 12-15, the Junior 2 category is many driver's first foray into a full-size racing kart. Larger rear tires, more complex chassis adjustment options, and yet more powerful engine options make the transition from Junior 1 to Junior 2 a significant step up in performance. (PC: Mark Lacour)

The Junior 2 category is a karting class that is usually available for drivers ages 12-15. In most cases, this class is a driver's first experience with a full-size karting chassis. This means that the Junior 2 category will challenge drivers to adapt to the physical, mental, and technical challenges presented by full-fledged performance karts. Like Junior 1, Junior 2 classes can have some variety in their actual name, which is largely dictated by the type of engine package that is run on the kart. Junior Rotax, X30 Junior, Junior Rok, and Junior Sportsman are all common names of sprint karting classes found across the country.

With a full size chassis, the capabilities of the driver and the racetrack can truly be fully explored. Most Junior 2 categories will use wider rear tires than on a cadet kart, which provides a significant improvement in grip and handling ability over kid karts and junior 1 karts. In addition, the sensitivity of a driver to the adjustments made to the kart, and their driving will be much more in demand, as the competition likely will continue to increase in quality and capability towards the front of the field. Most Junior 2 categories will place the weight of the kart and driver with safety equipment at 300-330 pounds. These karts can achieve speeds of 70-80 mph, with engine packages producing in excess of 25 horsepower at times.

Junior 2 drivers have an earned reputation for being slightly more aggressive than in Junior 1. Fortunately, this aggressiveness is often tempered by much more experience and patience than some driver's exhibit in the younger age classes. By the time many drivers enter this category, they have over 7 years of racing experience, and can begin to explore the subtleties of race craft and kart chassis setup. Many drivers that begin driving in this category quickly pick up on driving concepts and the feel of driving more readily than younger drivers, as their ability to listen to a coach or other drivers is significantly increased, as well as their bravery to try new things.

Like Junior 1 classes, Junior 2 races are riveting to watch when the turnout is large. Here, drivers in Junior Rotax race into turn 1 at the start of a race in Arizona. (PC: Musselman Honda Circuit)

Like Junior 1, Junior 2 classes are raced at the local, regional, national, and international level. If they wish to, a driver can travel the country and race against other drivers in similar equipment at a variety of racetracks, learning yet more about how to improve his driving and racing skills. The difference in driving styles from one motor package to another is also more pronounced in the Junior 2 classes than in Junior 1, which further enhances the growth of a driver, and allows them to get more driving or 'seat time' in a race weekend.

Once a driver has competed in Junior 2 classes for some time, or is ready to turn 16, they can enter the senior classes. As stated before, the specific age requirements within your region may differ slightly from the ages presented here, and it is always prudent to check with your local karting series and community about which class is right for you.

Senior

Once a driver is of the age of 16, they are ready to enter the senior karting classes. These classes feature some of the most experienced drivers, but also see many enter the sport for the first time. (PC: OnTrack Promotions)

The senior classes in karting are diverse, and above all else, without exception very competitive. As the previous karting classes may have implied, by the time a driver has risen to this class from kid karts, they will have potentially over 10 years of racing experience, which is enough time to have developed a truly impressive skillset. At the national or international level, the competition is incredibly close—1st to 15th can be separated by as little as 0.2 second! Don't be fooled into thinking, however, that by being a rookie with no experience at age 16 that you can't learn to compete as a senior-age driver!

Like the Junior 2 and Masters classes, Senior classes the world over utilize a full-size kart chassis. As a result, the adjustments, engine performance options, and tire compounds that senior classes can run on and utilize at the local or national level can be extremely diverse. In many of these classes, the engine has a displacement of 125cc, with horsepower ratings between 20 and 30 horsepower. In the highest performing karts, the shifter categories, the speeds these classes can reach exceed 100 mph. Most senior classes weigh between 325 and 360 pounds, with the driver and all safety equipment.

At the age of 16, most drivers are able to begin to self-inspect their own abilities with less guidance, a major change and improvement from younger drivers. As a result, both new and experienced drivers learn the skills that they need to become truly outstanding kart racers.

While not a universal class, some areas have an additional class beyond the senior categories for drivers aged 30 and above, typically known as the master class.

Master

Experienced drivers in the master classes tend to be smooth, experienced, and friendly racers. This is a good thing for drivers entering the category, as even the most competition-hardened master driver will usually be happy to talk about their driving. (PC: On Track Promotions)

While not a universal category, many karting series worldwide do have another karting class for drivers that are of an age 30 or above, known as the Master class. As the name implies, drivers that enter this category after spending years in senior classes have a supreme amount of experience. Or, if they are new to karting, these drivers are of an age that they want to experience the thrill of karting, but at an accessible amount of performance. Karts that compete in masters classes are still incredibly fast, capable machines, but with a slightly higher minimum weight when compared to the senior classes.

With the exception of the age of the drivers and the minimum weight of the kart, and on occasion the performance of the engine package, there are very few major changes from senior classes to the master classes. Many younger drivers look up to masters drivers, as many of them are driver coaches or mentors when they are not on the track racing themselves. Most masters classes have a minimum weight of 350-380 pounds, which includes the driver and all safety equipment.

As you now know, karting classes are separated primarily by the age of the driver, and the rough performance of the karting vehicle. This performance is driven by several factors that we have discussed, but one of the most important, the engine package, must be discussed in greater detail as its own topic: the engine.

In the next section, a thorough discussion of the different types of karting engines that one can see at the track will be carried out. Depending on the karting class a driver is set to compete in, there is almost certainly a specific engine package that all drivers within this class must utilize. This is done by karting series and organizations to keep the competition within each class close. As we will see, the engine packages, performance, and associated maintenance that each engine requires can be highly variable. Finding the right engine and class that fits your age, as well as your budget, takes a little research, which is best done initially by visiting your local karting series and racetracks.

The world of karting engines is, to put it lightly, one of the most varied and hotly debated areas within karting. Some competitors are strong proponents of engines that are durable, perform well, and are offered at an accessible price point for new and experienced karters. Other karters are strong proponents of extremely high-strung and 'high' performance engines. However, one thing that all karters do agree on regarding the kart engine is that without it, we would all be behind our karts, pushing them along. Whether a 4-cycle engine or a shifter kart engine, every engine package propels the kart along.

In general, kart engine package performance progressively increases in lock step with karting age classes. This means that the engines available for the kid kart classes are much smaller than those available for the senior classes. However, within each karting class there is a wide variety of engine brands, displacements, and overall performance that are held in favor within a certain region, series, and budget. As we dive into the world of engine packages, it is important to realize that while a certain engine may be the most popular within your local region, it is likely not as popular in other areas. The driving forces behind this significant region-specific focus are often complex and beyond the scope of this document, but it is important to note.

The performance, manufacturers, and accessories that are associated with kart engines is incredibly diverse. The particular engine that is in use in a racing series, class, or region is driven by many factors, and is not consistent across the world, or even a certain country. Finding the engine package that fits your region, budget, and type of kart racing can take some research. (PC: On Track Promotions)

Karting Engines

Since the beginning, go karts have been some of the lightest racing vehicles in all of motorsport. Initially, these light vehicles were powered by relatively heavy engines, if one considers the horsepower and overall performance these engines produced. While the single-cylinder, 2-cycle type of engine has been the most prevalent throughout karting history, the change that has taken place in kart engine technology over the decades has been remarkable. While early karts were still fun to drive, the race to build exciting, light, and more powerful karting engines began with the first kart races around parking lots in Pasadena.

The kart engines of today are the result of years of this push to build a better kart engine, full of experimentation, reform, and study. As time has progressed, the performance and accessories affixed to engines has changed considerably. Improvements in manufacturing processes, quality control, and performance technology has resulted in the replacement of the humble and underpowered lawn mower engines of years past with purpose built, precision-engineered karting engines. Regardless of the horsepower, accessories, or price of the engine, almost all karting engines are implemented in a certain class with the intent that every kart uses the exact same engine, built to the exact same or highly similar specifications. Ever-tightening restrictions, observant technical officials, and the organic inevitability of an engine package reaching a near perfect form means that parity within most karting classes can be largely achieved.

While you may not need one initially, many kart racers will utilize a motor builder or service technician to ensure that their engine package is within technical, wear, and service limits. Motor builders have the tools and knowledge to help you find the performance and reliability you need out of your kart engine. Here, a motor builder reassembles a carburetor after replacing some of the smaller gaskets and parts within it. (PC: OnTrack Promotions)

Today, karts compete with both 2-cycle and 4-cycle engines. Most of these engines mount to the right side of the kart in a specific region, and turn the rear axle by way of a chain drive and gears designed to match that chain. While all engines fundamentally do the same thing--propel the kart along—each engine package has its own power band, performance specifications, and parts that must be constantly monitored for proper function and mechanical state.

While the majority of this monitoring of an engine can be done by a karter after some initial instruction and education from a motor builder or other racers, it is often true that karting engines require regular more involved maintenance, inspection, and service. Depending on the engine, most will need an inspection, or a partial or complete rebuild after a certain amount of runtime hours. In most cases, these rebuilds and inspections are required to ensure that the engine does not become out of tolerance in many wear-critical areas, such as the cylinder wall, exhaust port, or cylinder head. Karting-specific motor builders and manufacturers often have qualified and helpful technicians within reasonable range of most karting facilities. These motor builders will take apart, inspect, and reassemble karting engines at regular intervals to ensure that the engines will produce the most power while also running efficiently. To many that are initially getting into karting, engine rebuilds and the maintenance required to keep many karting engines in perfect running order can be daunting. Fortunately, these motor builders service hundreds of engines each year, and can give you the basic understanding you need to work on and repair engine-related maladies in most situations. And, if the engine requires greater maintenance, most will perform the required service with the appropriate tooling and knowledge.

Kart engines of today are produced using advanced materials, manufacturing techniques, and computer-aided design to ensure that the greatest level of parity between each engine is achieved. In this photo, the CNC machines and manufacturing floor of an IAME Karting Engine factory is shown. (PC: IAME Karting)

In this discussion, we will separate the types of engines based off of their displacement, which is measured in cubic centimeters (CCs) of area to mix air and fuel in the bore of an engine. Broadly speaking, the displacement an engine produces is a rough indicator of the overall power output, and therefore the performance of the engine. This is why an engine of a 50cc displacement is typical of kid kart classes across the country, but 100 or even 125cc engine options are used in most powerful senior karting classes. While largely true, the adage of "no replacement for displacement" does have some exceptions to the rule. For example, in almost all circumstances a high-revving 125cc engine will be more powerful (and faster) than a 206cc Briggs & Stratton LO206 engine. In these cases, factors such as the power band (operating RPM range), gearing, and even carburation must be considered. For some car enthusiasts, it should also be noted that karting engines are normally aspirated even without the use of turbochargers or extremely complex additional components, most kart engines still perform within RPM ranges that are considered ludicrous for most larger-displacement engines found in racecars or an automobile.

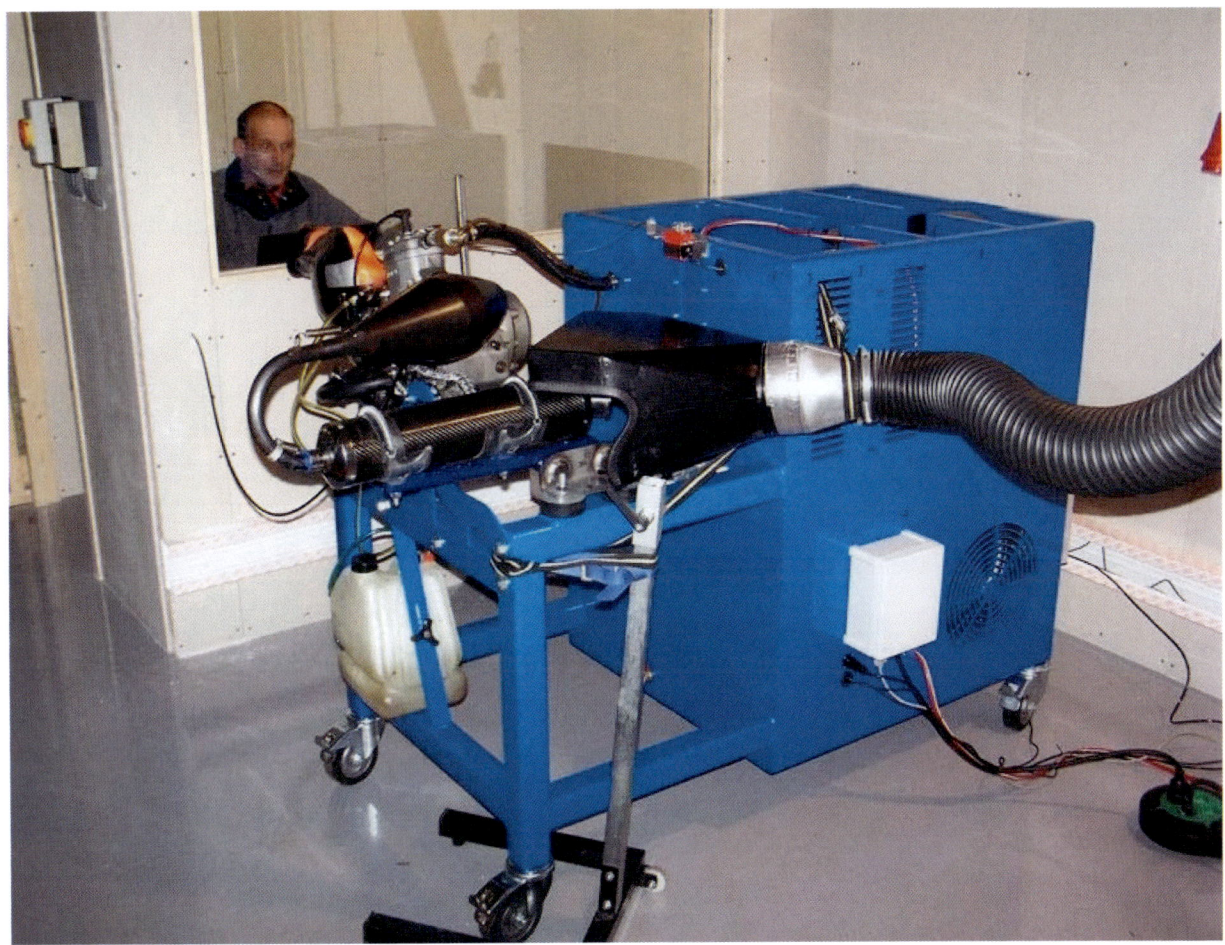

Many kart manufacturers and motor builders will utilize an engine dynamometer similar to the one depicted. These 'dynos' allow karters to simulate the stresses and strain of the engine during competition in a controlled environment, to ensure that the engine package can deliver top-level performance. (PC: Radne)

A quick note: while this section will focus primarily around 2 cycle engines, which are common in sprint kart racing, it should be noted that the same principles apply for 4-cycle engines—the more displacement, the higher the resultant performance. **While many engine packages are presented in the following pages, a trip to your local kart track or racing series will give you the best insight into the engine packages commonly used within your region.**

50cc engines

In recent years, the Honda Gxh50 engine has been the go-to engine package for most Kid Kart classes across the country. 50cc engines produce between 2 and 4 horsepower, and will propel a Kid Kart to a top speed of roughly 40 mph. (PC: Ekartingnews.com)

As one would expect, a 50cc engine is considered to be on the lower end of the performance scale of karting engines. While other displacements and engine package options are available, the 50 cc engine is the most common displacement for engines used in the Kid Kart class. These engines produce between 2-4 horsepower depending on the technical specifications that have been set forth by the racing series or karting organization they compete in. This is enough power to propel most drivers to a top speed of 40 mph. While some 50cc engines can be 4-cycle, most are still 2-cycle engines.

Like all other karting engines, power is delivered from the engine to the rear axle by way of a chain drive and a rear and front sprocket. The sprocket that attaches to the engine is often referred to as the 'driver sprocket,' and is typically made of hardened, heat treated steel. These engines typically operate at temperatures that are relatively low, and therefore they are almost always air cooled. As the kart moves along, the wind resistance against the engine cools the engine and clutch, keeping key components cool enough that they do not overheat.

In another feature that is common to most karting engines, 50cc engines utilize a centrifugal clutch. This clutch transfers power from the engine to the drive train (chain and sprockets) by expanding internal components slightly once the throttle is applied. At a certain rpm range, the components within the internal area of the clutch expand, grab onto the 'drum' that the driver sprocket is attached to, and the rear axle turns as the chain drive turns.

As mentioned earlier, most 50cc engines are 2-cycle in nature. This means that the oil and fuel must be mixed in the gas tank prior to combustion in the engine, to ensure proper lubrication and operation of the engine components. This mixture is known as 'pre-mix,' a combination of castor oil and racing fuel, which has a higher octane rating than most pump gas. Depending on the engine, karting series, and their ultimate regulations, the fuel, oil, and engine package that a class may run will vary. The technical specifications of how much oil and fuel that should be mixed together depend on several factors, and it is best to consult with your local karting series or service shop before conducting this mixing. Improper mixing can either rob performance from the engine, or severely damage the engine if not enough lubrication via castor oil is used.

While not as fast or capable as their 'big brothers,' 50cc engines are still considered performance engines. Experienced kid kart drivers learn to master the idea of 'momentum conservation,' and will still drive through corners with considerable speed. (PC: Road & Track)

In some cases, 50cc engines can be slightly modified to gain more power within a set of technical guidelines, known as technical specifications for the engine. Examples of modifications that *can* be allowed include widening of the intake and exhaust ports, honing or machining of the cylinder bore and head, and alteration of the carburetion or ignition settings. **Before you do any of these things, however, always consult with the technical experts on hand at your local track, karting series, or regional sanctioning body representatives. Improper modifications, whether intentional or unintentional, can be grounds for disqualification, or damage the engine.**

60-80cc Engines

For many years, the next major step up in displacement (and therefore performance) was the 80cc karting engine. Most famously, the go to, hands down reigning champion of 80cc karting engines used worldwide was the 80cc Comer K-80, the engine that earned 'cadet' karting classes the moniker of "Junior 1." Today, however, the landscape of 60-80cc engines is slightly more diverse. In many premier karting organizations in the United States and Europe, the 60cc engine displacement is becoming more popular. The most common application for karting engines of a displacement between 60 and 80cc is for Junior 1 classes, but *some* are used with either de-tuned or 'extra-powerful' modifications for the Kid Kart and Junior 2 classes. In most cases, the bottom line is that 60-80cc engines are intended for drivers of ages 7-12, and primarily therefore will be featured in the Junior 1 classes.

The particular engine that is in use at your local karting club can vary significantly depending on the region in which you are located. However, the Parilla Mini Swift, Comer K-80, Briggs Junior LO206, Rotax Micro Max, and Yamaha KT100 are the most popular options for sprint kart racing in most of the world that deliver the level of performance commonly found in the junior 1 classes. While each of these engines may have specific technical requirements, most have a broadly similar performance ability: 6-12 horsepower. With these engines, a 'cadet' kart can reach speeds in excess of 80 mph on certain tracks. More commonly, however, most maximum speeds will be between 50 and 70 mph.

Unlike the 50cc engines, which are mostly 'pull-start,' a 60-80cc is most commonly started by an electric starter motor, or by the use of an external starter. This is done because the cylinders of these engines tend to hold more gases and fuel for compression, and the feasibility of pull starting these engines becomes more challenging and hard on equipment. Once the engine is started, most engines require some time to reach operating temperature. Even on the hottest days, you may see 60-80cc engines being run on the kart stand for extended periods of time prior to going out on the track.

Most 60-80cc engines are air cooled, but some do use a small radiator to cool the engine to enhance the durability and wear patterns of the engine package. While almost all 60-80cc engines utilize a centrifugal clutch, some utilize a gearbox with a more robust, hand-operated clutch. These engines are most commonly found in the 80cc shifter kart categories, which is a class and engine package that has come and gone from popularity in karting several times over the years.

Like the 50cc engines, most 60-80cc engines are 2-cycle. This means that the oil and fuel must be mixed in the gas tank prior to combustion in the engine, to ensure proper lubrication and operation of the engine components. This mixture is known as 'pre-mix,' a combination of castor oil and racing fuel, which has a higher octane rating than most pump gas. Depending on the engine, karting series, and their ultimate regulations, the fuel, oil, and engine package that a class may run will vary. The technical specifications of how much oil and fuel that should be mixed together depends on several factors, and it is best to consult with your local karting series or service shop before conducting this mixing. Improper mixing can either rob performance from the engine, or severely damage the engine if not enough lubrication via castor oil is used. If an engine is 4-cycle, then pure racing fuel is used, with regular oil changes required that are separate from the fueling process.

In recent years, 'Touch and Go' type engine technology has migrated from higher-power classes to the 60-80cc engine. Examples of these include the Parilla Mini-Swift (pictured) and the Rotax Micro Max. Here, a Mini-Swift engine package is shown in disassembled form. From left to right: Battery box and wiring loom, exhaust (background), engine, air intake and filter. (PC: Comet Kart Sales)

It is often the case that 60-80cc engines can be slightly modified to gain more power within a set of technical guidelines, known as technical specifications for the engine. Examples of modifications that *can* be allowed include widening of the intake and exhaust ports, honing or machining of the cylinder bore and head, and alteration of the carburetion or ignition settings. In other cases, the engine is to be a 'spec' engine as delivered from the factory. Engines that fit this rule set mentality include the Rotax MicroMax, and the Briggs Junior LO206. **Before you do any of these things, however, always consult with the technical experts on hand at your local track, karting series, or regional sanctioning body representatives. Improper modifications, whether intentional or unintentional, can be grounds for disqualification, or damage to the engine.**

100cc engines

A legacy of karting's earlier development, the 100cc engine displacement category has been mostly usurped by 125cc engines. However, exceptions still exist in karting. Initially implemented in the early 1980s, the 100cc Yamaha KT100 engine package is famed for its durability and close racing action. Of all 100cc engines, this package is the most common still in use today. (PC: Oscar King)

The 100cc engine displacement size has been the backbone of most adult karting classes for most of karting history. In recent years, 125cc engines have mostly taken over this honor. However, 100cc engines can still be found in many karting classes and series, and therefore bear coverage and explanation here.

The 100cc engine package represents a significant step up from the 50cc and 60-80cc engine package categories. Rather than 8-12 horsepower, many 100cc engines produce in excess of 18-22 horsepower, and can reach higher RPM ranges (12-15,000 vs. 6,000-11,000 for a 60 cc engine). Like other karting engines, 100cc engines can be either air cooled or water cooled with the addition of a radiator. It is still fair to say that most 100cc engines are air cooled, however, as most have significant cooling fin work around the internal portions of the engine. Like other engine packages, they can also be started by the use of an onboard starter, or by an external one that turns the crankshaft until the motor fires.

Like many 60-80cc engines, a 100cc engine is usually highly sensitive to the ambient temperature, humidity, and altitude that are present during a karting competition. Many kart racers are familiar with how to adjust their carburetors, spark plug, and fuel mixtures to gain the most performance out of these engines in a variety of conditions.

In a departure from some 60-80cc engines, almost all 100cc engines deliver their power by the use of a centrifugal clutch. As you may recall, it was mentioned that 80cc engines can utilize a gearbox. In most cases, a 100cc engine utilizes a dry 'disc-type' clutch that serves as the interface between the power of the engine and the turning of the rear axle and wheels.

Like the 50cc and 60-80cc engines, most 100 cc engines are 2-cycle. This means that the oil and fuel must be mixed in the gas tank prior to combustion in the engine, to ensure proper lubrication and operation of the engine components. This mixture is known as 'pre-mix,' a combination of castor oil and racing fuel, which has a higher octane rating than most pump gas. Depending on the engine, karting series, and their ultimate regulations, the fuel, oil, and engine package that a class may run will vary. The technical specifications of how much oil and fuel that should be mixed together depends on several factors, and it is best to consult with your local karting series or service shop before conducting this mixing. Improper mixing can either rob performance from the engine, or severely damage the engine if not enough lubrication via castor oil is used. If an engine is 4-cycle, then pure racing fuel is used, with regular oil changes required that are separate from the fueling process.

It is often the case that 100cc engines can be slightly modified to gain more power within a set of technical guidelines, known as technical specifications for the engine package. Examples of modifications that *can* be allowed include widening of the intake and exhaust ports, honing or machining of the cylinder bore and head, and alteration of the carburetion or ignition settings. In other cases, the engine is to be a 'spec' engine as delivered from the factory. Engines that fit this rule set mentality include the IAME Ka-100, and the Briggs Junior LO206. **Before you do any of these things, however, always consult with the technical experts on hand at your local track, karting series, or regional sanctioning body representatives. Improper modifications, whether intentional or unintentional, can be grounds for disqualification, or damage to the engine.**

With increasing regularity, inspections, rebuilds, and replacement of 100cc engines created rising cost issues for many karting competitors. As a result, 125cc engines have become the norm for many classes in which a 100cc engine was utilized in the past. While they usually have more components and fixtures associated with them, the 125cc engines tend to be more reliable, and create greater parity among competitors than some 100cc engine packages.

125cc Engines

125cc engines come in many forms. However, as you can see from this photo, most 125cc engine packages are significantly more complex than their smaller displacement siblings. Pictured is the componentry of a 125cc IAME X30 engine, one of the go-to Touch and Go (TaG) engine packages on the market and in use today. Note the larger exhaust, radiator (at top of picture), radiator hoses, wiring loom, battery box, and large air intake and filter. (PC: Comet Kart Sales)

In many ways, the 125cc displacement engines represent the most diverse set of engine packages in karting. The engines used in karting that are 125cc is highly varied, and is subject to local, regional, and international influences. In most applications, 125cc engines are utilized in the senior and master age classes, for driver 15+. This, however, is beginning to change, with the advent of the 'de-tuned' 125cc engine in some younger age classes, like the Rotax Mini Max or Junior Max. While most 125cc engines are 2-cycle, some can be 4-cycle.

With exceptions like 'de-tuned' 125cc engines like some Rotax engines set aside, most 125cc engines produce anywhere from 20-30 horsepower, and operate in RPM ranges that are often higher than their small-displacement counterparts—12,000-20,000 RPM. In the most extreme case, a 125cc, 'ICC' shifter kart can rocket to speeds of 110+ mph on certain tracks. Most 125cc engines will propel karts along at top speeds of 75-90 mph, however.

While exciting to watch, a shifter kart engine is typically the most complex and temperamental of all engine package types in karting. In their most extreme form, the ICC shifter engine, driving one becomes as much about hanging on as it does about being smooth and relaxed. (PC: On Track Promotions)

Unlike the karting engines we have seen so far, *most* 125cc engines are water cooled. This of course means that they utilize a radiator. The size, placement, and usefulness of a radiator varies from each 125cc engine package. Fundamentally, they all serve one purpose—to keep the engine within operating temperatures. For most 125cc engines, this is usually between 130 and 200 degrees Fahrenheit. In addition, many 125cc engines are dubbed 'Tough and Go,' or "TaG" motors, because they have an electric start system. This system includes a battery, wiring harness, ignition modules, and of course, the starter. Strangely, it should be noted that not all engine packages that are technically TaG engines are referred to as such around the paddock. For example, a Rotax is a TaG engine—after all, it has a starter, radiator, and battery. However, almost everyone will call a kart powered by a Rotax engine a 'Rotax kart,' rather than a TaG kart. While confusing, it is a quirk of the karting culture, and will likely remain as such. It should be noted that higher performance 125cc engines that are found on shifter karts are almost never TaG engines. These will require a push to start. Some skilled drivers will run alongside their kart, jump in, jam it in gear, and take off. Most require a mechanic to push them.

From what you have read so far, it may become clear that you can divide 125cc engines into two fundamental categories: TaG (Touch and Go) engines, and shifter kart engines. Both are typically water cooled, produce significant horsepower, and are used in senior and master classes predominantly. However, there are significant difference between the two main types of 125cc engines. Most notably, many TaG-type engines utilize a centrifugal clutch that is similar to those used in lower engine displacements. Shifter karts, however, utilize a more traditional method of

43 | Karting 101: An Overview of Competitive Kart Racing

controlling how power is delivered. While shifter karts still use a clutch, it is no longer 'automatic.' Rather, it is designed to be used via a hand-actuated clutch lever. Most shifter kart engines are derived from (or at least inspired by) the 125cc engines that were initially used in dirt bikes—the Honda CR125 being the most direct example. While exciting to watch, a shifter kart engine is typically the most complex and temperamental of all engine package types in karting. In their most extreme form, the ICC shifter engine, driving one becomes as much about hanging on as it does about being smooth and relaxed. Many drivers describe driving a shifter kart as controlled chaos, and they do love it!

Like the 50, 60-80, and 100cc karting engines, most 125cc engine packages are 2-cycle. This means that the oil and fuel must be mixed in the gas tank prior to combustion in the engine, to ensure proper lubrication and operation of the engine components. This mixture is known as 'pre-mix,' a combination of castor oil and racing fuel, which has a higher octane rating than most pump gas. Depending on the engine, karting series, and their ultimate regulations, the fuel, oil, and engine package that a class may run will vary. The technical specifications of how much oil and fuel that should be mixed together depends on several factors, and it is best to consult with your local karting series or service shop before conducting this mixing. Improper mixing can either rob performance from the engine, or severely damage the engine if not enough lubrication via castor oil is used. If an engine is 4-cycle, then pure racing fuel is used, with regular oil changes required that are separate from the fueling process.

It is often the case that 125cc engines can be slightly modified to gain more power within a set of technical guidelines, known as technical specifications for the engine package. Examples of modifications that *can* be allowed include widening of the intake and exhaust ports, honing or machining of the cylinder bore and head, and alteration of the carburetion or ignition settings. In other cases, the engine is to be a 'spec' engine as delivered from the factory. Engines that fit this spec-rule set mentality include the Rotax Max range of 125cc engines. Examples of engines that are slightly more 'open' in the 125cc category include the Honda CR125, The IAME X 30, and Parilla Leopard (the engine that is most commonly dubbed with the TaG nickname). **Before you do any of these things, however, always consult with the technical experts on hand at your local track, karting series, or regional sanctioning body representatives. Improper modifications, whether intentional or unintentional, can be grounds for disqualification, or damage to the engine.**

200+ cc: 4-Cycle Engines

The 4-cycle karting engine has been in use in oval kart racing for decades. It is only recently, however, that the 4-cycle engine has been widely used in sprint kart racing. Note the drive train location, large size of the engine, and split rear sprocket. (PC: Acceleration Karting)

Since the beginning of karting, 4-cycle engines have been utilized in all major forms of karting, but at varying levels of extent. While not the dominant form of engine package in sprint kart racing, many forms of kart racing utilize 4-cycle engine packages exclusively. In particular, oval kart racing and many endurance karting series have evolved with the 4-cycle engine as a constant presence. For several decades, 4-cycle engines were often replaced with lighter, more powerful 2-cycle engines in sprint kart racing. In recent years however, improvements in manufacturing quality, cost savings, and parity among 4-cycle engines have seen them return to prominence in many sprint kart racing series. In particular, the Briggs & Stratton Local Option (LO) 206 package has taken sprint kart racing by storm, and is considered one of the main factors for a resurgence in 4-cycle kart racing on a national and international level. While the performance and power of each 4-cycle engine can vary, most produce between 8-20 horsepower, and will propel karts along at 40-80 mph.

Just like their 2-cycle siblings, 4-cycle engine packages used for karting come in a variety of styles, variations, and of course, performance levels. It should be noted that while the core concept of more displacement = more performance is still mostly true when discussing 4-cycle kart engines, this does not mean that all 4-cycle engines are stronger than their 2-cycle counterparts. As mentioned before, many 2-cycle kart engines with less displacement will be faster on the same kart than a 4-cycle engine with a larger amount of displacement. The horsepower, top speed, and life cycle of the two fundamental types of engines (4 and 2-cycle) are vastly different in many cases.

Just like their 2-cycle counterparts, 4-cycle engines can be 'de-tuned' to work well for a variation of karting age classes. Here, a group of 4-cycle powered karts compete in the Junior 1 category in Colorado. (PC: Gia McNerny)

At the heart of the difference between a 2-cycle engine and the 4-cycle engine is of course the increase in the number of cycles of the crankshaft a 4-cycle engine requires to produce power. While both 2-cycle and 4-cycle engines of today employ advanced materials and technology to produce their impressive performance, a 4-cycle engine simply requires more components, and therefore more weight, to function: A camshaft, valves, and associated valve train componentry are present in each 4-cycle engine. As a result, every 4-cycle engine tends to slightly larger than their 2-cycle counterparts.

Most 4-cycle engines are air cooled. This means that each engine relies on large surface areas to be utilized to cool the combustion chamber, rotating components, and general case of the engine. This cooling is aided by the large abundance of oil that is present in each 4-cycle kart, which is channeled and re-cycled throughout the engine in a much more efficient manner than in a 2-cycle engine. Many 4-cycle engines will run best at an operating temperature considerably higher than their 2-cycle counterparts: 300-400 degrees. While this difference may seem extreme, remember that the componentry and design of most 4-cycle kart engines are designed to sustain these temperatures without appreciable parts failure. While some high-performance 4-cycle engines can be water cooled with the addition of a radiator and hoses, it is not terribly common to see at the track regardless of karting series or type of karting competition.

While 4-cycle engines are becoming more prevalent in all types of kart racing, the premier example of the potential of 4-cycle engine packages in karting has consistently been oval track karting events. Almost all oval karts are powered by 4-cycle engines. (PC: TKA)

In most cases, 4-cycle engines utilize a chain drive and front and rear sprockets to deliver their power to the rear axle, and propel the kart along. However, the location for these components is typically on the opposite side of the motor than a 2-cycle engine. This means that the clutch, sprockets, and chain are located to the left of the engine, rather than the right, if the kart is viewed from behind. In oval kart chassis design, this is already accounted for and understood. However, on many sprint kart chassis, this change can result in some additional finagling and work required to accommodate the components of the drive train. Aftermarket kart parts manufacturers have rapidly responded to this change by making aftermarket accessories for fitting most 4-cycle engines to most karts.

Like many other karts, most 4-cycle kart engines utilize a centrifugal clutch. Due to the vibrations and additional torque many 4-cycle engines induce on the drivetrain of the kart, 4-cycle clutches often look more substantial than their 2-cycle counterparts. However, they both function in the manner. While rare, 4-cycle shifter karts do exist, and these karts have a small gearbox just like their 2-cycle counterparts.

As you may have surmised, 4-cycle engines do not require mixing of racing fuel with oil prior to its introduction into the engine—a common practice on all 2-cycle kart engines. For many racers, this is a nice feature of the 4-cycle engine. However, this advantage is tempered by the fact that most 4-cycle engines will require regular oil changes. The extreme heat and torque that a 4-cycle kart engine produces is challenging for even the most advanced oils to handle. As a result, it is not uncommon to change the oil more than once per day at a serious racing event. On most practice or testing days at the track, however, many karters will only change the oil once.

In a trait that is unique to 4-cycle kart engines, some karting series or engine packages can be powered by fuels other than gasoline. In some applications, alcohol-based fuels such as methanol are used to lower the sustained engine temperature while also producing outstanding performance. In such a case, specific materials, tolerances, and accessories are usually fitted to the engine that differ from the 'stock' technical specifications. While these fuels have their advantages, they can also be more temperamental. The altitude, ambient temperature, and carburetor and ignition settings under which fuels other than racing gasoline work can be tricky to optimize.

It is often the case that 4-cycle engines can be slightly modified to gain more power within a set of technical guidelines, known as technical specifications for the engine package. Examples of modifications that *can* be allowed include widening of the intake and exhaust ports, honing or machining of the cylinder bore and head, and alteration of the carburetion or ignition settings. In other cases, the engine is to be a 'spec' engine as delivered from the factory. **Before you do any of these things, however, always consult with the technical experts on hand at your local track, karting series, or regional sanctioning body representatives. Improper modifications, whether intentional or unintentional, can be grounds for disqualification, or damage the engine.**

As you can see, karting age classes and varying engine performance packages exist to separate drivers into categories that allow them to race with others of similar ability. While it is certainly true that a new driver that just turned 12 may not be best suited to race in a national-level race in the junior 2 class right away, he or she likely would find the adjustment to the kart performance and challenges present at a local karting race in the Junior 2 class within his ability. In this manner, karting has organized itself to accommodate both new and experienced racers as they progress in age and ability.

Now that a discussion of the basics of go karts, types of racing, and how karting events are separated by classes and engine performance, it is time to talk about the races themselves. After all, one does not go from a complete newbie to national champion in any sport overnight! Like most other sports, karting has competition at local, regional, and international levels. Finding the series and level of competition that is right for you will likely mean beginning at a local karting club, but understanding the various competition options available will likely help you make the most informed decision.

In the next section, the varying levels of karting competition will be discussed. Again, this discussion will focus primarily on the structure present in the United States, but the same structure is present elsewhere.

Karting offers various levels of competition. Local, regional, national, and international karting events are held by sanctioning bodies and racing series all over the globe. Here, an karting series official signals competitors during a race. (PC: OnTrack Promotions)

<u>Kart Racing Series</u>

Like karting classes, there are discrete levels within karting competition that a new racer should likely know about before they begin karting. Like many sports, it is unlikely the most positive experience for a new competitor to enter a national-level event, and expect to be instantly competitive. Fortunately, karting has strong local organizations that allow for racers to experience the sport at a fun and accessible level. In addition, regardless of the level of karting competition, racing officials are a permanent presence at the track. These officials ensure that races are conducted safely and efficiently.

For some, a regional or even national event may be within their reach in terms of experience or finances very quickly. For most that are new to karting, however, local karting clubs and racing series are where drivers cut their teeth, and learn the basics of kart racing. In this section, a basic overview of the various competition levels will be carried out. While this discussion will primarily focus on the karting scene in the United States, local karting clubs and regional racing series exist all over the world. In addition, a brief overview of the officials you can expect at any karting event will be conducted. Before going to the track for the first time to witness a race, knowing who to look for can make your experience that much more informative.

49 | Karting 101: An Overview of Competitive Kart Racing

Local Karting

Local karting series and racing clubs provide the first step for most people when they begin racing karts. For many, a season club championship is a major goal, and the friends they make along the way become lifelong.
(PC: Gia McNerny)

For most racers, the place to begin competing in karting events is with a local racing series, or karting club. Typically, these clubs race at only one or two tracks, usually within the same state. In many cases, multiple karting clubs coexist within one region, providing more opportunities for dedicated karters to race against new competitors, and at different racetracks. Like all karting series, club events feature multiple classes that are separated by age, engine package, and kart performance. If you have not read our section on karting age classes, now would be a good time to do so.

While the turnout at these series can vary by region, most karting clubs typically feature 60-150 participants across a wide array of karting classes. Many of the drivers that run at the front of local races are quite experienced at a particular track or set of racetracks. They are usually happy to talk to new racers, and give them some tips about how to navigate that particular racetrack. On occasion, regional or national racers may visit local karting clubs to brush up on their skills, prepare for a racing series that will be coming to that racing venue soon, or simply to race and enjoy local karting.

Most local karting series or clubs are run primarily by volunteers, many of them karters themselves. While volunteers, most have extensive racing experience, and are able to point new members of their club in the right direction. In addition to providing the best place for new racers to compete in a safe and constructive environment, local karting clubs actively work with new racers to ensure that they understand and learn all important signals and event procedures everyone must know to partake in karting events safely, and with respect for other racers. Most local races are one day in length, with open or official practice sessions available the day before the event at the racetrack that hosts the competition.

Regional Karting

Regional karting series are considered a step up from a local karting club or series in terms of competition. In most cases, the racers have some experience. While not international champions, they will learn together how best to race, and, eventually, consider racing for national titles. (PC: Gia McNerny)

In most cases, regional karting events are considered a significant step up compared to local karting series or clubs in terms of competition. Many regional series will race at more than one racetrack, and, in many cases, more than one state. Naturally, a regional series may have a certain regional emphasis. As an example, the International Karting Federation's Region 4a conducts karting races across multiple tracks in the state of Colorado.

Regional racing is often the first chance for kart racers to experience a different racetrack than their 'home' track, where they may have hundreds if not thousands of laps. While there is no set rule for when it is time to make the move to join and participate in a regional racing series, most local karters will decide to compete at a regional event, see how it goes, and then decide to spend more time racing locally, or dedicate themselves to a regional effort. At many regional series, the turnout is close to that of a local kart series, but can at times swell to in excess of 200 entrants across the racing classes if a series is particularly strong.

Regional karting series are often some of the strongest and most consistent karting events in terms of competition. In many cases, a national or international driver will return to regional racing series because they know they can consistently find great competition. (PC: Gia McNerny)

With increasing occurrence, a regional racer will begin to notice their competitors make the journey to national competitions, often succeeding or running well. Each regional series has a sense of pride in the karters it produces, and even if not in attendance at a national event, the 'home' racers are always encouraged to do well. Regional karting is one of the most stable levels of competition to enter as a new or developing racer, as there will likely always be someone at your skill level to challenge and push you. Unlike local karting events, many regional events have more than one day of competition. Most competitors attend practice days before the event, to familiarize themselves with the local track, and tune their driving and karts.

For many, a regional karting championship represents a master stroke in their racing career. For others, however, the call of larger fields, even tighter competition, and new racing venues can be a serious reason to consider national karting competition.

National Karting

National karting is a challenge for every racer. Whether a 15 time national champion or a newcomer to national competition, every racer that competes at the national level can likely learn from others. (PC: OnTrack Promotions)

For most, the transition from regional to national karting competition is one of the biggest challenges they will face in their karting career. At any national event, there are multiple regional standouts, many of whom already have years of racing experience, championships, and accolades to their name or team. As with most sports, it is recommended that you have significant experience before investing your time, money, and sweat at a national event.

Unlike local or regional racing events, national karting events are only held a handful times each year. An example of a series that has multiple national level races in a year would be the SKUSA Spring or Summer Nationals. An event that is a standalone national race would be the IKF Sprint Grand Nationals. In another deviation from regional or local races, these national events typically take place at well-known tracks across the country, and the venue changes every year, rather than returning to the same tracks and region multiple years in a row.

Many national karting drivers compete with larger teams, which support particular karting brands, or products. Through national events, these drivers are often instrumental in improving the performance of various karting equipment, be it helmets or a kart chassis. The racing action is often enthralling but also cutthroat, with contact between drivers not only occurring, but expected.

While national events may only come along a handful of times each year for most racers, national competitors are constantly practicing, looking for ways to improve their driving, and chances of success come race day. Often, teams will travel to the venue ahead of hand, spending multiple days or even weeks at a track, refining their chassis setup to be ready. Data analysis, expert kart tuners, and experienced motor builders are all key components of most winning national kart racing efforts.

International Karting

International karting competitions are some of the most spectacular and challenging events in all of karting. The SKUSA Supernationals is a yearly event, and hosts drivers from all over the world in several classes. Each class features immensely prepared and experienced racers, brought together to win a premier international karting event. (PC: On Track Promotions)

For many drivers, a national title is the pinnacle of their karting achievements. In many cases, a driver may have developed their skills to the point that they find national competition compelling in its own right, or are ready to transition to another form of motorsports, or continue to race at a high level in karts. In other cases, however, a driver may journey to race internationally. Many of these karting competitions are the result of nationally-recognized 'ticket' programs, which give drivers an opportunity to represent their team or even their country at international events.

By design, the track, other competitors, and even the chassis are usually complete unknowns to most international karting competitors prior to entering an event. This of course means that the very best drivers, mechanics, and team members will rise to the top in these events. Unlike a national karting event, the chance to extensively prepare is erased, and so a driver's natural talent, work ethic, and racing luck will largely dictate his ultimate finishing position.

While most karting competitors may never experience an international karting event, it has been a staple of karting competition from the early days of racing. Through these international competitions, the challenge, friendships, and culture of karting can be shared with others from different regions worldwide. Some lasting effects of these competitions for karters in the US include the prevalence of European (primarily Italian) karting chassis being used in competition in the United States, and the Team USA Scholarship, which selects multiple talented karting prospects each year to compete in Europe through a structured program. While many international competitions are held outside of the USA, the SKUSA Supernationals is considered to be a premier worldwide karting event, and attracts international participants each year.

Karting Officials

Whether at an international or local kart race, there are key officials and people in place to ensure that each and every karting event occurs in a safe and fair manner. Without these people, there simply cannot be kart racing. Often the first to the track on race day and some of the last to leave, kart race officials serve in a variety of roles and accomplish a multitude of key tasks each race day. While some are relatively new to the world of karting, many have years of experience, procedures, and rule sets in place that govern their decisions, and actions. Regardless of the series, level of competition, or official role, every karter knows that kart race officials are to be treated with respect, and ultimately trusted to make the correct calls throughout the day. In this section, we will quickly touch on some of the key players you can expect to see at any karting event.

At any karting event, the race director is in charge of ensuring safe and fair competition conditions, and enforcing penalties if a competitor behaves in an unsafe or unsportsman-like manner. Here, a race director (in red) talks to drivers about the changing track conditions, likely reminding them that they must adjust their driving for rainy track conditions. (PC: OnTrack Promotions)

First and foremost, at any karting event you will likely find at least one trained paramedic. These paramedics are on site from the moment a kart rolls out onto the track, and will not leave until all competition for the day has occurred. Equipped with all the medical supplies, experience, and training they need to respond to karting-specific incidents, they are ready at a moment's notice to respond to any incidents that have taken place on track. In addition, they will address anyone that has become ill in the paddock. While a medical response to an incident on track is not terribly common, these paramedics are ready to respond to incidents within seconds of occurrence. In almost all cases, these emergency medical technicians (EMTs) have multiple radios that allow them to communicate with all necessary personnel and officials that conduct the racing events, ready to pause an event if they need to respond.

At almost all karting events, staff is also on hand to stand out near the race track in key positions to assist race participants in the case of an accident. While most are known as corner workers, this position is also known as a corner marshal in some countries. These marshals typically are instructed to respond to accidents, give reports of on-track behavior, and enforce penalties or warnings within their region of interest around the racetrack. Most stand to the inside of the racetrack when possible, in positions that allow them to be safe from most racing action, but also visible in case they must signal to competitors in the event of an accident, or officiating decision. Corner workers must be quick, agile, and alert, as they are the first responders to any incident on the racetrack. Most are in constant radio communication with other officials, namely the race director.

Depending on the event, the race director may also be the head flagman. However, in most cases, they stand alone, constantly watching the race proceedings. He or she has earned their position, the result of years of experience as a kart participant, official, and from having a general knowledge of the sport. As with any sport, karting has both written and unwritten rules that are to be adhered to on and off the track. These rules include but are not limited to the sporting conduct, mechanical state, and passing decisions a driver or kart makes. The race director has the ultimate authority and judgment to make officiating decisions. These decisions can be, but are not limited to: advising, warning, and in some cases, disqualifying participants if their behavior is deemed to be out of line or unsafe, whether intentional or unintentional. In many cases, a penalty may be handed down to a competitor from the race director for something that is not entirely in their control, but is unsafe, like a component on their kart coming loose during a race, or their safety equipment being improperly secured. While race directors do not enjoy enforcing most rules, they do take their jobs extremely seriously, and should not be disturbed during racing events, as they are responsible for the safety and integrity of racing competition. Just like the corner workers, race directors almost always have a radio or headset in hand, ready to give directions to those that need them.

Technical or 'Tech' officials are on hand at almost all kart races. Often some of the most experienced karters at any event, they are in charge of overseeing that the rules, integrity, and fairness of competitions are enforced. To do this, they sometimes need to do a little disassembly. Note the instruments, gloves, and apron in this photo of a technical inspector at work. All tools of the trade! (PC: OnTrack Promotions)

Before the race day even begins, registration assistants and membership assistants are at the track. They have the proper forms, paperwork, and payment processing equipment to ensure that you enter the racing venue with the proper vouchers, wristbands, and credentials. In most cases, a race track that hosts a karting event will require all participants to sign a liability waiver, and pay for an entry wristband. In addition, certain areas of the pit area or supporting parking are organized based on the safety and accessibility for all participants. Without these registration assistants, the safety of competitors on the track, as well as the general members of the pits could be in jeopardy, or at the very least be extremely disorganized.

Regardless of the event, technical directors are some of the most experienced and knowledgeable people at the track regarding the mechanics and performance of karts. The technical director is in charge of inspecting karts before and after racing events, and enforcing penalties for technical infractions. In some special cases, technical directors are also in charge of determining if track conditions regard mandatory pauses in competition to allow for cleaning of the track, or ending a race prematurely. The technical director always has a concrete rule set of technical specifications, dimensions, and parameters that they will hold all competitors accountable to, regardless of finishing position, budget, or experience. These range from ensuring that ballast is painted a bright color (white or orange), enforcing penalties for being below minimum weight for a karting class, or even the displacement of the engine on a kart. In most cases, technical directors will advise competitors about general technical questions, as they want competitors to be within all rules before they finish a race, when a penalty could really hurt them. In some cases, technical inspections can take considerable amounts of time. At a regional, national, and especially at international events, trained and certified technical officials will be in attendance, with special tools and high accuracy gauges on hand to check any number of dimensions, tolerances, or performance parameters. Many a kart racer has attempted to guess what a tech inspector may check at a race, and almost always they are caught if they attempt to cheat.

At many events, you may also encounter grid marshals. Like corner workers, these men and women are on the front lines at most karting events, organizing racing events as they come along in the schedule for a day's activities. These officials work to make sure that karts line up in the correct order for racing events like qualifying, heat races, and of course the final races. This ensures that no one gains an advantage inadvertently, and serves to ensure that all competitors are ready to roll out onto the track when their event is scheduled.

A kart race announcer must balance keeping the event on schedule with covering the on track action. While a local or regional race may not attract a significant amount of spectators, national and international karting competitions benefit strongly from a color commentating team that brings a level of excitement that other sports feature.
(PC: OnTrack Promotions)

While not always present at a race, an announcer is one of the most omniscient presences at any karting event. I say this because, if they are there, you hear them throughout the pits through the speakers arranged around most karting tracks. An announcer may tell racers of the time available until their race is next on the track, if competitors must come to a meeting, or if inclement weather necessitates racing action to be put on hold. While their main function is to announce upcoming events to competitors throughout the paddock to ensure that the race day is run smoothly, they also have given karting some of its most memorable moments. Their fervent and frenzied tone while commentating can at times drive other competitors from their chairs in their pits to the fence, to witness a particularly fierce battle, cheering as a driver makes a masterful pass, or takes a well-deserved victory. At national and regional karting events, announcer often interview drivers, which gives younger competitors their first taste of professional public speaking.

Kart racing officials work to ensure that events are run efficiently and fairly with respect to all competitors, regardless of experience level. Here, a tech official waits near the scaling area for competitors to come off the track. (PC: On Track Promotions)

So far, we have covered quite a lot! If you have read thoroughly, you now understand what makes a kart perform as it does, the main types of kart racing, the ages classes of karting, the types of engines available, and levels of karting competition that are available. But, what about *you?* After all, you still need to understand what gear you may need to begin karting yourself! In the next section, we will discuss the safety equipment every racer needs to have before turning their first laps in a kart.

While no one wants or expects to have an accident, crashes are part of any form of motorsports. Often, the cause of an accident is not your own doing: a part can fail, a competitor can spin, or you can make a driving error. Safety equipment keeps you protected when these things happen. (PC: On Track Promotions)

Safety Equipment

Like many other sports, karting requires that certain safety equipment is worn to be allow competitors to have fun while also being safe. Unlike other sports, karting occurs at a high rate of speed, in machines that can (and do) make contact with each other, or their surroundings. When they do, the required pieces of karting safety gear every driver wears work together to keep them safe. **This section is a must read for any and all potential karters! It is in your best interest, as well as the safety of others, to never, ever scrimp on proper safety equipment.** While karting accidents are statistically rare and injuries often relatively minor, accidents can and do happen.

This section is devoted to a general overview of the karting-specific safety gear every driver is expected (and in almost all cases, required) to wear anytime they are going to drive a kart. In the following section we will discuss the gear that you need to drive a kart safely. This includes a racing suit, a helmet, racing shoes, and full-coverage gloves. While not mandatory in some cases, a neck brace or support system, a rib vest, and at times, padding may be suggested safety additions that can prevent serious injury or discomfort. **If a driver is under the age of 15, they will almost always be required to wear a neck brace or support system, as well as a rib vest with an additional chest or "sternum" protector.** This is for their safety, as most young children are still developing in the rib cage area, and the extra protection mitigates injuries.

60 | Karting 101: An Overview of Competitive Kart Racing

While not a common occurrence, karts can overturn. When researching your own safety gear, consider a situation like this. Here, this driver's helmet, neck protector, rib vest, and suit all work together to cushion the impact this driver is experiencing. Within moments, a corner worker and likely a paramedic will be at his kart to pull him free. (PC: OnTrack Promotions)

As you wander around the paddock at a track, peruse the internet, or talk to a brand representative for safety gear on the phone, you will likely encounter more than one strong opinion when it comes to safety gear. Some will say you should only spend a certain amount on your first set of safety gear. Others will say that you should only buy the best, most expensive, most certified and popular safety gear. Clearly, the answer that is right for most competitors lies somewhere in the middle of all of these sentiments. However, regardless of your ultimate purchasing and brand decisions, one thing is always true: Safety should be your first priority when you decide upon what gear you **will** wear. Note that I said *will*, not 'consider,' 'think about,' or 'decide upon later.' Karting is a fun sport, but it is serious when it comes to safety.

I, and almost everyone you meet at the track, is serious about safety. Your first and foremost habit that you should develop upon entering a karting facility is to **consider your safety your responsibility**. Without question, almost all accidents that do occur would have had much worse results if all competitors were not wearing their required safety equipment. Karting series, other competitors, and sanctioning bodies take a very dim view on those that defy, ignore, or circumvent safety requirements because of a perceived advantage, or due to stubbornness.

Without further belaboring the point of why you should wear all the required safety equipment, it should also be noted that without it *you will not be allowed on the track.* While many karting facilities have some safety equipment for sale or rent for your first karting experience, almost all competitors in karting, whether at a local or national level, own and take care of their own karting safety gear.

By design, karts do not usually have a roll cage or seat belts installed in them. In an accident such as this one, the driver is considered safer by falling out of the kart than remaining squarely in the seat, where the full weight of the kart could be placed upon his head and neck. In this accident, a driver's rib vest, helmet, and suit keep him safe from the kart and the abrasion of the track. (PC: OnTrack Promotions)

In the following pages, each key piece of safety gear that every karter should wear is explained at a fundamental level. It should be noted that the ratings, fit, and style of equipment that is right for you can vary significantly. **It is in your best interest to thoroughly research each item on your own, and decide upon each item after careful considerations in regard to the performance, cost, and feel of the gear.**

Helmet

The karting helmet of many elite karting drivers is a place to express their own style with unique and compelling paint schemes. Regardless of the color, style, or price, one thing is universal to helmets: they all are intended to protect the most vital and important part of a driver's body: their head. (PC: On Track Promotions)

The use of a helmet in karting is by far the most important thing one can do to take the right first step to protecting themselves in case of an accident. While the type, brand, and even size of a helmet will vary based on personal choice, required safety standards, and budget, a helmet is hands-down the biggest piece of gear every karter must have. After all, our brain is an important and vital organ. While resilient, as humans, our heads are not engineered to sustain some of the impacts one can expect in a karting accident without some protection. Years of research and improvement have resulted in the full-face helmets of today.

A full face, certified and inspected helmet is required for all karting competition events. Karts do not have a seat belt, and that is by design. In the case of a flip, it is best for drivers to fall out of the kart so that it does not land atop them. Without the driver, a kart can weigh in excess of 250 lbs, which is a considerable amount of weight to land atop someone in the case of a flip. In the worst case scenario, a full face helmet will adequately protect a driver in minor and major impacts should their kart flip in an accident. In addition to impact protection, a helmet serves to protect the driver from long skids or slides along pavement, gravel, or other track side materials. While unpleasant, this not a particularly dangerous experience for drivers that wear helmets.

Like most racing drivers, karters tend to be fiercely loyal to one particular brand or style of helmet. Ultimately, seeking advice about what helmet is best for you must be tempered with considering what helmets are commonly used in competitive karting, and which deliver the best protection. (PC: On Track Promotion)

The ratings that are required for karting competitors can vary from the the local, regional, and national level, and of course the general geographic region of competition. In the United States, common certifications that all organizations like to see include the DOT, Snell 2015, and ECEE certifications. Particularly, the Snell certification indicates that a helmet is rated for and will perform well in motorsports competition, and in accidents that may happen to a kart driver. **To find out which helmet certifications you will likely need to meet, the best method is to consult a karting rulebook, which all karting series and events will have at their disposal.** Many are available online, and are the result of years of research and karting know-how to ensure that basic rule sets are followed and can be adhered to at each event.

Like most safety equipment, the fit of a helmet is critical to its proper function and performance. While this guide will not (and should not) be a definitive guide for finding the proper helmet fit for you, a helmet should fit tightly, and feel as though it is an extension of your head when you turn, rotate, or jostle your neck and head. That is to say, the helmet should fit tightly, and conform comfortably to your head shape.

Many helmet brands, sizes, and options are available, which ensures that a helmet that fits within your budget, head size and shape, and application. While the style and size of your helmet is something that you may be able to narrow in on by looking online or talking to some experts, **you should always try on a helmet before you purchase one**. Other factors you should consider when purchasing a helmet include visibility, breathability (the venting on the helmet), the history and ratings of that helmet or brand, and the materials from which it is constructed.

Suit

A karting suit is designed to be first and foremost abrasion resistant. Unlike racecars, karts do not catch fire very often. As a result, a karting suits primary function is to prevent against abrasion from wind, debris, or in some cases, the track itself. Here, a driver in a full karting suit gets a push start from his mechanic. Imagine the protection that driver would have if he only wore what his mechanic does! (PC: OnTrack Promotions)

While karting suits may look slightly strange at first, it will soon become something that you can trust and rely upon to protect you in accidents. Karting suits are somewhat unique in the four-wheel motorsports world, in that they protect primarily against abrasion. For this reason, some karters call kart suits 'abrasion suits.' Unlike their fire retardant counterparts, these suits are primarily useful in accidents where a driver scrapes, bumps, or touches another kart or the racing surface in an accident. As a result, the materials and design of karting suits is intended to handle extensive abrasive forces against them in an accident. Because fires are incredibly rare in karting when compared to racecar accidents, most karting suits are not designed to be fire retardant, although a few have been tested to be.

The rating system for karting suits is similar to helmets. Although DOT ratings can exist for some racing suits, primary rating systems for karting suits include the FIA rating, and local ratings that are not quite as universal. SFI, a large presence in motorsports certification in the United States, has tested some karting suits before, but primarily tests for racecar suits, rather than karts. If you are considering buying a used suit, and see an SFI rating, be careful. As stated before, while these suits can be helpful in an accident, they will likely not have the abrasive performance of a karting-specific suit.

While you may see some people wearing 'half-suits' at the track, and blue jeans (or god help them shorts) when driving at a local practice day, don't consider these people to be the ultimate authority on safety. While better than nothing, any motorcycle rider can tell you how well jeans hold up in a high speed crash. Some oval karting racers do use blue jeans as safety gear, and in those applications it may be adequate, as a full body kart does protect the driver somewhat. Regardless, a full coverage, karting-specific suit is required for most karting competitions and series.

While this guide is not intended to (and should not) be a source of the best advice on what suit works well for you, a racing suit should fit so that it covers your extremities fully. This means that the 'cuffs' of the suit cover up until your ankles and wrists. This best ensures your safety in a crash. While a suit may feel comfortable near the waist, if it pinches at your neck or shoulders, it is likely a little too tight, or short. If both of these areas feel comfortable, and the suit is not exceptionally loose or baggy on your body, then it is likely an adequate fit. As you become more comfortable with karting, your personal preference for fit and comfort may drive you to choose a certain brand.

In inclement weather such as rain or sleet, a karter may want to wear a rain suit. These plastic suits fit over the normal karting suit, and keep the competitor dry and warm. Most do not offer additional safety protection, however. (PC: OnTrack Promotions)

Shoes

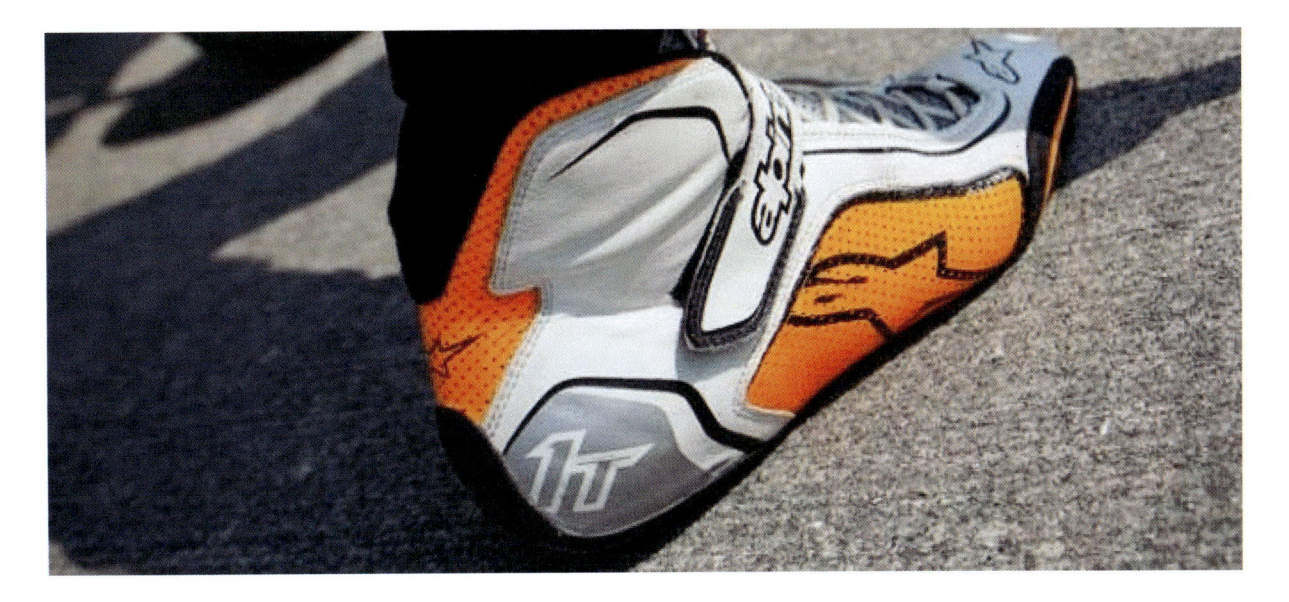

Like karting gloves, shoes serve to protect the driver, but also to give them the best driving feel. Note the protection and padding around the ankle, rolled shape of the heel, and top Velcro strap to ensure a tight fit, and keep laces from wandering where they shouldn't. (PC: On Track Promotions)

Solid safety gear for your feet with additional over-the ankle protection is a must. Unlike their street-worn counterparts, racing shoes typically have a very thin sole and a rolled heal, both of which improve throttle and brake application. While the choice of racing suit should be based off of comfort and fit, it is required that the shoe be a 'high-top' style. The 'high-top' protection is critical in many karting accidents, as the ankle area is often susceptible to significant movement laterally into hard objects like pedals. Having the extra protection around your ankles protect you from these accidents, and also provide extra support should your foot hyper-extend or drag in some accidents.

Like all shoes, racing shoes should fit tightly, but not constrict feeling in the toes. A classic 'toe test' of pinching the front of the shoe is always in order when fitting new racing shoes. Often, it may feel difficult to fit racing shoes at first, as the heal area is often extremely curved when compared to many normal shoes, and can be surprising to those that have not worn racing shoes before.

For younger drivers, a nice pair of high top shoes can be worn in lieu of racing specific shoes. While child sizes are made, finding the right fit can be a challenge, and outside of some people's initial budget. If a young racer can tolerate or likes a pair of Chuck Taylor high-tops for his first driving shoes, then these can be allowed in some cases by a racing series. It goes without saying, but loose shoelaces, extra padding, or anything that may interfere with the use or action of the shoe as it was intended are heavily discouraged based on common sense and safety.

Gloves

Gloves ensure a driver's hands are properly protected, and also serve to give drivers the best feel for the kart as they drive. Note the fitment of the 'gauntlet' of the glove over the karting suit, which is how they should be ideally worn. (PC: D&M Motorsport)

Karting gloves are an important investment for the protection of your hands, and also for proper driving feel. Without gloves, the gravel, dust, and debris that can be kicked up in normal karting competition can damage a driver's hands. It is also very common for calluses to build up on the palms of a driver's hands if gloves are not worn, due to the cornering forces felt in a kart.

The fit and feel of a pair of gloves can often take time to refine to your own liking, as the feel of the steering wheel through the gloves must be as precise as possible. For most, a glove that feels comfortable around the juncture of the lower arm bones (radius and ulna), as well as over their knuckles, is likely sized properly for that driver. If the glove pinches or binds near the wrist joint, or in the knuckle area, the glove is likely either too small, or does not suit your hand type.

Karting gloves should cover the hand completely, as well as beyond the wrist. The lower part of the glove (the 'gauntlet') is important for extra protection in a crash, and should be wrapped around the suit to ensure that in a sliding accident a driver's arm or hand cannot accidentally get exposed. Gloves are made by a variety of companies, in all sizes, with a variety of materials composing them. Common materials used in gloves include leather, hybrid textiles, and even Kevlar. If properly used, gloves are one of the most important pieces of safety equipment in karting, and also one of the most important to your overall health and comfort level during and after driving any kart.

Rib Vest, and Chest Protect

While this vest is designed for a smaller driver, one can see how it basically functions. A set of side pads and protectors wrap around the torso of a driver, the shoulder straps providing support. The pronounced bulge at the front of the vest is an integrated chest protector, which is one of the best safety innovations to come to karting safety gear in the modern era. (PC: SharkShifter)

A rib vest and chest protector are two of the best investments anyone can make to keep themselves safe and comfortable throughout their karting career. Because karts do not have suspension, padded seats, or many other 'comfort' amenities that are found in most vehicles, a kart can truly put a toll on your body if one does not take the proper steps to protect their body with devices like the rib vest. Setting aside the serious protection these devices deliver in an accident, most karters enjoy wearing them, as without them, bruises or soreness of ribs is a common problem. This problem is particularly exacerbated on rough or extremely grippy racetracks, or in higher-horsepower karts.

In an accident, the padding and hardened plates that are found in ribvests protect your sides, back, and chest from severe impacts, particularly against the fiberglass or plastic seat of a kart. These ribvests are typically worn beneath a driver's suit, but some do wear them on the outside of their suit—it is really up to your personal preference. Most fasten at the front with multiple plastic clips, which can be adjusted to fit your particular chest and torso dimensions, in a similar fashion to the straps on a backpack. Ribvest companies typically provide the consumer with very detailed sizing charts, which ensure the buyer that they get one that will fit properly.

For most drivers, a ribvest should fit in a snug, encompassing manner. This means that while it should not feel like you are being strangled around your ribs, you should not feel like you are wearing a loose fitting jacket either. A great way for most to test for proper fit is to put the rib vest on, adjust the straps until it feels about right, and then deeply inhale to 90 or 95% of their lung capacity. If your body and chest feels confined and slightly uncomfortable through this action, then the vest is likely about as tight fitting as it should be. This feeling should be uniform around the body, and not in one particular zone or region. If on exhalation the feeling persists, then the vest is likely adjusted too tight, or is too small. The shoulder straps of the vest should push down lightly on your shoulders, but again, should not constrict your arm movements or neck muscles substantially.

As mentioned in the introduction to this section about karting safety gear, **a chest protector is required for drivers under the age of 15 in most karting series and applications**. To gain further insight on this, contact your local karting series, or track. These chest protectors often resemble armor plating, and this is for good reason. Often, they will Velcro to an existing rib vest, or affix to the driver in an 'x' cross pattern of straps. This protects younger drivers from impacts in frontal collisions on objects like a steering wheel or motor. As someone who has hit both of these objects in accidents at a younger age, I am a staunch advocate for the use of the chest protector by drivers of all ages.

Neck Protector

A neck protection device is designed to mitigate hyperextension or unnatural movements of the head and neck in severe accidents. Improvements in design over the years have resulted in the protection devices seen today. Note how the construction of the device conforms to the curves of his shoulders, back, and the curvature of the base of his helmet. This is an example of a helmet and neck device being designed to work together, which is critical for a neck protection device to function properly. (PC: OnTrack Promotions)

Neck protectors are sometimes the most controversial piece of karting gear a new karter may consider buying. **Like the additional chest protector, for almost all younger drivers, a neck protection device of some kind is required.** For drivers over the age of 15, they are often optional. When these were first developed, they were little more than foam collars, designed to resist the natural rotation and hyperextension of the neck in karting accidents. Over time, these protection systems have become more advanced, and made of stronger materials such as plastic, carbon fiber, and other composites.

While not as common in karting anymore, a foam collar can be worn in some cases to meet the required safety guidelines for a karting series. Most of the time, the drivers that are wearing them are either experienced karters that are used to wearing them, or newer drivers that may not have the budget to invest in the more expensive (and likely better performing) neck protection devices. Initially, these were developed by a company called Leatt, so many may still call them "Leatt braces." Today, products that provide similar levels of protection are made by several companies.

A foam neck collar is considered by many to be good, but likely not as comprehensive in most accidents as modern neck protection devices. Here, a modern example of a neck collar is shown. Note the large lip of material on the rear of the collar, which is an improvement on older designs, and somewhat limits hyperextension of the head and neck rearward. (PC: RaceDay Safety)

Upon closer inspection of a neck protection device, a new driver or karter may notice the strange contours, overlapping sections, and oddly jutting pieces. The neck protection system typically relies on sitting flatly on the frontal chest, upper back, and shoulders of a driver. When testing for the fit of a particular device, realize that the more interaction and contact the device has with these areas of the driver, the better it will perform in a crash. Many of these devices have considerable adjustability built into them, which allows for this fit to be correct. Consult with a sales representative or experienced karter who has extensive experience fitting and using these devices before purchasing one.

At this point, we have covered the essential, 'need to know' sections surrounding karting. A fundamental overview of the go kart, age classes, engines, karting competition levels, and safety gear has been conducted. Whether you have read this document thoroughly, or perused only the portions of it relevant to your age, experience level, and favorite type of kart racing, hopefully you have gathered some general information that is useful to you in your next steps in karting.

Hopefully, this means it may soon be time to go to your local track or kart shop, and see some karts in person! This likely means you may encounter the kart racer in their natural habitat: in the pits, a kart shop, and of course, on the track. As a result, a discussion about some of the associated equipment and tools each racer may want to consider having before they begin karting is necessary.

In the following section, a discussion will be conducted regarding some of the basic tools most karters have in their toolbox. It should be noted that this discussion will not be all-encompassing, and will likely omit some tools that a lot of your local racers have that is particular to their style of kart racing, chassis brand, or even to their mechanical abilities. In addition, a quick overview of some of the pit equipment common to karting will be conducted. While it is easy to argue that a kart stand or fuel jug could just be lumped into a discussion about general tools for every karter, these pieces of equipment are considerably more sizeable and expensive than a small open end wrench.

For many racers, it is important to also understand what options they may have for transporting their kart to and from the track. Therefore, a quick overview of transportation options will be entertained towards the end of this section.

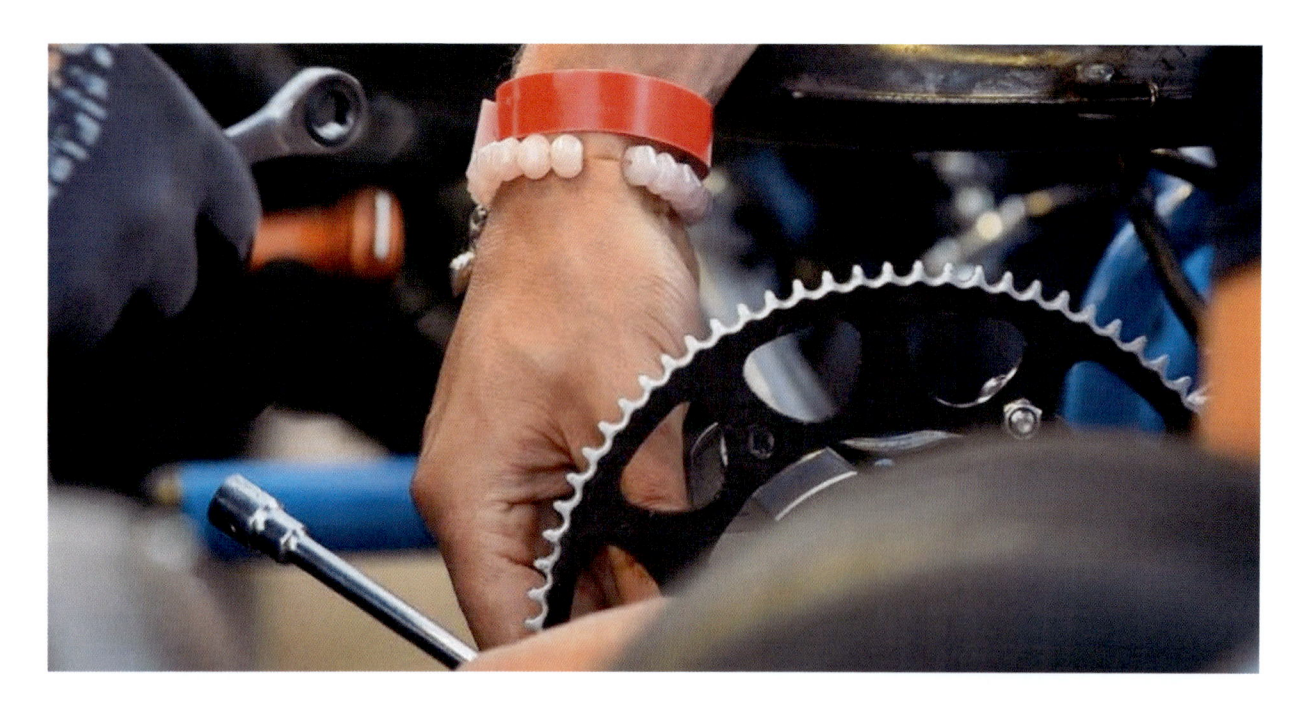

Regularly maintaining the components of your kart is about more than keeping them in functional order. By regularly making a habit to inspect your kart from stem to stern, you can catch loose or worn components before they become a major issue, and cost you time on the track or from finishing a race. (PC: OnTrack Promotions)

Karting Maintenance: Tools and Equipment

As you may have guessed by now, the know-how to care for and maintain a kart can present a learning curve to new racers initially. Unlike a baseball bat or soccer ball, a kart does not fit easily in a small closet, and requires significant attention to keep it in perfect working order. Like any other vehicle, a kart must be owned with the understanding that it requires regular maintenance, inspection, and service if you wish the vehicle to perform as desired. In this section, a discussion about the equipment and tools that can be used to keep karts working properly will be carried out. Your karting experience will be greatly enhanced by making a habit of regularly maintaining and preparing your kart for a day at the track.

Depending on the type of kart, engine, and the performance you require from it, the associated maintenance can vary significantly. Many introductory karting classes or series will feature karts, engine packages, and tires that require less maintenance and expenditure than those that compete at a national or international level. However, even local karting competitions require regular kart maintenance. This maintenance includes regularly cleaning the kart and components, changing tires, and servicing and inspecting engine components. Because most karts are considered high performance machines, the stresses and strains induced on karts can be quite extreme. By regularly maintaining your kart, you can expect it to stand the best chance of standing up to these stresses while also delivering the desired level of performance.

Without exception, all karters work extensively on their racing machines. At first, your focus may be on just keeping the kart in running order. Soon, however, the focus will be on finding more speed by adjusting the kart's chassis settings, tinkering with the engine, and of course, improving driving. (PC: OnTrack Promotions)

As a general overview regarding the key components of karts and the various types of engine packages has been conducted already, this discussion will focus on the items most kart racers or owners may have in their pit or shop when they work on their karts. While some kart racers elect to have others work on and care for their karts for them away from the track, the vast majority of karters own their own kart and equipment, and perform most maintenance themselves on weekends, evenings, or at the track on race day. Properly preparing for success by maintaining your kart is the key to improving your karting experience, and your performance on the racetrack.

While many maintenance and repair tasks surrounding your engine package can be done by most karters with basic hand tools, some maintenance tasks require specialized equipment and extensive labor to accomplish. As mentioned in the engine section of "Karting 101", motor builders have the precise knowledge, machining skills, and testing and analysis equipment to improve the performance of your kart engine, and keep them in top shape. As a result, this section will focus on the tools most racers have at the track to perform the general kart maintenance that is required to keep karts in perfect mechanical order, not on involved processes like rebuilding an engine that is (at least initially) best left in most cases to an experienced motor builder.

This discussion regarding karting maintenance and tools will be separated into three main sections: pit/shop tools that most karters should have, karting retailers, and transportation options.

General Tools and Equipment

Having the right tools to work on your kart is just as critical as having the proper safety equipment when you're on the track. Without the tools to service all the components on your kart, you can be severely hindered on race day or during a practice session. (PC: OnTrack Promotions)

Whether at the track or in your garage, having the proper tools to work on your kart is a great first step to being able to prepare and maintain your racing machine for every track day and racing event. Because go karts are manufactured all over the world, the basic tools you may want to work on your particular kart can be both of the American standard and metric type. In addition, sometimes more basic tools such as hammers or screwdrivers are handy to have. While not always necessary for a new karter, battery-powered tools like a drill or impact gun are common fixtures of many karting toolboxes.

For most sprint karts, many components that are native to the kart will likely be metric, as the kart was likely manufactured in Europe. However, many oval track karts are entirely made in the USA, and therefore fasteners and components will require standard wrenches, sockets, and allen-head wrenches. Another factor that may affect the tools you would want to have on hand can be some of the aftermarket components you have associated with your kart. Some examples of these could be motor mounts, pedals, and of course, the engine.

As a result of the varied fasteners on any kart, most racers will have a supply of both types of basic hand tools at their disposal. For most karters, it is recommended to have a solid set of open

76 | Karting 101: An Overview of Competitive Kart Racing

end wrenches sizes 2mm to 19mm for metric fasteners. For most standard fasteners, wrenches between 1/8" and ¾" are advisable. Because of the tight clearance margins and applications of some fasteners on all karts, allen-head or 'hex-key' fasteners are extremely common. Therefore, having a set of metric and standard allen keys is another must-have to work on your kart. In addition, both phillips and flat-head type screw drivers are a must to be able to work on most engine components associated with delicate electronics, or many carburetor components. Having a good tape measure is also a good idea, as it can help you make fine adjustments to your kart to improve its handling or performance. Sometimes, a component may hang up, become bent, or need some 'fine adjustment.' In these cases, having a range of hammers and pry bars can be helpful. Many karters have a weighted rubber mallet in their toolbox, which is useful for changing an axle, or straightening a bent component after an accident.

As you begin to work on your kart, you may find that certain wrenches or fasteners require the most attention. As a result, many karters have a set of 'common use' tools at the top of their toolbox, easily available to quickly handle most maintenance tasks. In addition to the basic hand tools listed above, many racers use power tools to speed up their mechanic work. As a result, a cordless drill or impact gun is a recommended tool to have, for jobs like tightening wheel lug nuts, or removing major components in a hurry.

If you don't have a specific tool right away, don't worry! Especially at local karting events, most racers are willing to help you learn to work on your kart. Some may lend you a tool, or show you how to work on specific components. While most racers may not be as forthcoming with tool help or kart chassis tuning advice once you gain some experience, it is not at all uncommon to see multiple teams coming together to help another racer after a major accident. These teams may use their combined knowledge, tools, and manpower to accomplish seemingly impossible repair tasks in an impressive amount of time.

Other tools that karters may want to have at their disposal are much more kart-racing specific. As an example, the tires on a kart require regular attention. One of the major adjustments a driver can make regardless of the type of kart racing is the tire pressure present in the tires on their kart. While the exact tire pressure you may run will depend on many factors like the track temperature, tire brand, and compound, one item that is almost assured to be in any kart racers toolbox will be an accurate tire pressure gauge.

A tire pressure gauge is a popular basic tool to have at the kart track. While most are not as fancy as the electronic unit pictured here, a pressure gauge is a must-have for karting. (PC: On Track Promotions)

Initially, you may be able to get by with a standard air gauge you can find at most auto parts store. Over time, however, a racing-specific gauge is likely something you will invest in. While some karting facilities have pressurized air on hand for the use of all competitors, many karters will have a small air compressor on hand for their use at the track. Others opt to use compressed tanks of nitrogen, which is known to be more stable and consistent as it builds and loses heat and tire pressure. Regardless of the gas you use to fill your tires, letting most of it out to change tires is done by removing a bead-lock on your kart rim, or the valve-core in the vale-stem of the tire. As a result, many karters also have a valve-core tool, which resembles a small flat-blade screwdriver. Once the air is out of the tire, a bead breaker tool, tire tongs, and even a tire changing machine may be necessary to change the tires you have on your rims, which are reusable just like on a car. Many tires are soft and small, which means that a skilled kart racer may be able to change them by hand once the tire is de-beaded. For most, this is a skill that can be learned, but may not be the best to do immediately. In many cases, other karters at the track can give you the best advice about where and how to get your tires changed when starting out.

Another karting-specific tool that is common for every karter to have at the track is a kart stand. Kart stands come in many forms, but are generally made of welded and bent steel components, with the purpose of supporting the kart at an elevation of 3-4 feet above the ground. Small casters or larger rubber tires allow for easy transportation of the kart to and from the racetrack to your pit area. Once at your pit, a kart stand makes it much easier to work on the kart, both from above and below. Many will fold to some extent, which makes them easier to store and transport to and from the racetrack. While more expensive than a standard kart stand, some 'one-man' stands are available, which lower down to the kart on ground level, and then hydraulically or mechanically lift the kart upward to a normal height. Some also come with a small shelf or area to place parts, tools, and gear at an arms-reach when working on your kart. In recent years, a vertical kart stand has been a common piece of equipment that many karters use for storing their kart, as it makes the kart fit nicely in many trailers or storage areas.

Few karting tools or pieces of equipment are as helpful as a kart stand. These stands make it easy to move the kart from your pit to the grid, and work on the kart with little hindrance. Many stands, like the one pictured, have a small tray for tools and parts, and can fold or collapse to be easier to transport. (PC: On Track Promotions)

A 5-gallon fuel jug is a very common sight in most karting pit areas. These fuel jugs are usually made of durable plastic, and can be somewhat transparent, or mostly opaque. While most racing fuel is sold in a metallic 5-gallon pail at a karting retailer, the convenience and weight of a plastic fuel jug makes it an easy choice for most racers to be driven to purchase one. Most have gallon gradations on the side, which makes precise fuel-oil mixing an easy process. If you do purchase one, consider a flexible filler nozzle as an additional extra, as it makes fitting the fuel into the narrow neck of most kart fuel tanks much easier.

Other karting specific tools you may want to consider purchasing at some point (likely not right away) may not be used extensively at first, but will become highly beneficial as time continues on. One of these includes a front-end alignment system. These systems come in several forms, but one of the most common is a system known as the Sniper laser alignment system. This allows kart racers to set the alignment of their front wheels, which is critical to ensure proper tire wear, chassis performance, and as a reference to check if components of the steering system have become bent in an accident.

At almost every karting event, you will see many fuel jugs around the pits or near the track. These fuel jugs provide a safe and convenient method to store and transport racing fuel. At some national events, these jugs are required to remain in a controlled area of the pits, so that extra tampering or alteration of competitor's fuel cannot take place. (PC: OnTrack Promotions)

While there are many more karting tools a racer may want to consider purchasing that pertain to maintenance of their kart, the last major one that we will cover in this section is a data acquisition system, or a simple lap timer. In your initial journey to a track, you will likely see many of these affixed to karts around the pits or on the track. Some are only simple lap timers, which sense a beacon at one point around the track each lap, usually placed at the start/finish line. This allows a driver to get instant feedback regarding their performance on the track, and their laptime. Other systems are extremely complex, with readings available for the engine temperature, kart speed, RPM, and even position on the track via GPS. While these systems can vary in price, all of them are a fantastic tool to gain instant feedback and data about your driving and kart performance!

A data acquisition system like this one, pictured attached to a driver's steering wheel, is highly useful for many reasons. Depending on the functions the system has, a driver and kart's lap time, RPM, engine temperature, and even GPS position on the track can be found within the data these systems store or display in real time.
(PC: OnTrack Promotions)

It is inevitable that some tools that you may need or encounter at the track will not be covered in this section. However, regardless of the type of kart racing, budget, or level of competition, the tools listed are likely to be present in each and every pit.

As mentioned before, getting all the tools you need to complete every maintenance task on your kart right away isn't always possible. Over time, each karter develops their own methods and tools that they like to use to accomplish similar tasks. Asking others for some advice if unsure how to perform a certain task can usually be constructive for both parties, as an experienced karter may gain a better understanding of a process by explaining it. With that said, **don't forget that the mechanical state and performance of your kart is ultimately your responsibility**. While others may be willing to lend a hand or a tool from time to time, the expectation among karters is that you are in charge of the general maintenance and service of your kart the majority of the time.

While it is great to know about the various basic tools you may want to have before you begin kart racing, what about parts and service? After all, karts have components on them that commonly need replacement due to wear, accidents, or for performance. In the next section, a quick overview of karting retailers will be carried out.

Karting Retailers

Karting retailers can often be found at karting facilities across the country. Many of these retailers will partner with national or even international brands, manufacturers, and parts suppliers to have a large selection of karting-related parts, apparel, and inventory in stock (PC: OnTrack Promotions)

Like any sport, karting has a dedicated group of merchants and experts located near racetracks across the world that have the parts, apparel, and general karting knowledge that can be helpful to both the experienced and new karter. In many cases, a particular karting retailer, colloquially known as a 'kart shop', will support a particular set of chassis brands, international parts suppliers, or even produce products themselves. Kart shops serve as the front line for parts and experience that you can count on when you head to the track, and are constantly re-stocking their inventory to be able to continue to serve the karting community.

While heading to your local track can be helpful to get a visual exposure to karting, a trip to a local kart shop can also provide you with an opportunity to inspect, handle, and discuss various karting-specific tools or accessories prior to your initial purchase. As a new kart racer, some of the things that a kart shop may be particularly helpful with would be explaining a certain chassis, inspecting a kart engine, or helping you try on and sample a variety of karting safety equipment or tools. In some cases, kart shops can provide storage for your kart, or perform advanced maintenance or repairs of existing parts. While not always the case, many kart racers tend to form a relationship with a certain kart shop in their area, and will remain loyal to those that help them take their first promising steps into the sport.

Now that you have some familiarity with the general tools and general retailers, it may be time to consider transportation options for getting these pieces of your karting experience to and from the track. In this next section, a brief overview about transporting your kart will be carried out.

Transporting a Kart

While many karters may start with a pickup or SUV to transport their first kart, eventually their friend or family member may want to take part. For most, this means purchasing a small trailer, which protects the karts from the elements and theft in style to and from the track. Here, the use of vertical kart stands vastly improves the available space in this small trailer (PC: Fast100karting.com)

Transporting a kart to and from the track can be one of the most challenging obstacles that many new karters may face. After all, not everyone has the budget to go out and purchase a large trailer with all the bells and whistles, let alone have space to park it! While there are many that do pursue this option, for others the transportation of a kart can be done in the back of a pickup truck, and even in most midsize or large SUVs.

In almost all cases, go karts are approximately 6' long, and slightly less than 5' wide. While this is not true of all karts and you should *always check a karts dimensions before you choose a transportation option,* it is a good rule of thumb for most karts, regardless of discipline. In the case of an endurance or laydown kart, these karts are likely to be slightly longer (7 or 8'), but also slightly more narrow. With some minor disassembly, many karts can be made to be significantly smaller than these rough dimensions. By removing the front and side bodywork, wheels, and even the rear hubs, a kart can shrink considerably in overall footprint in an instant.

83 | Karting 101: An Overview of Competitive Kart Racing

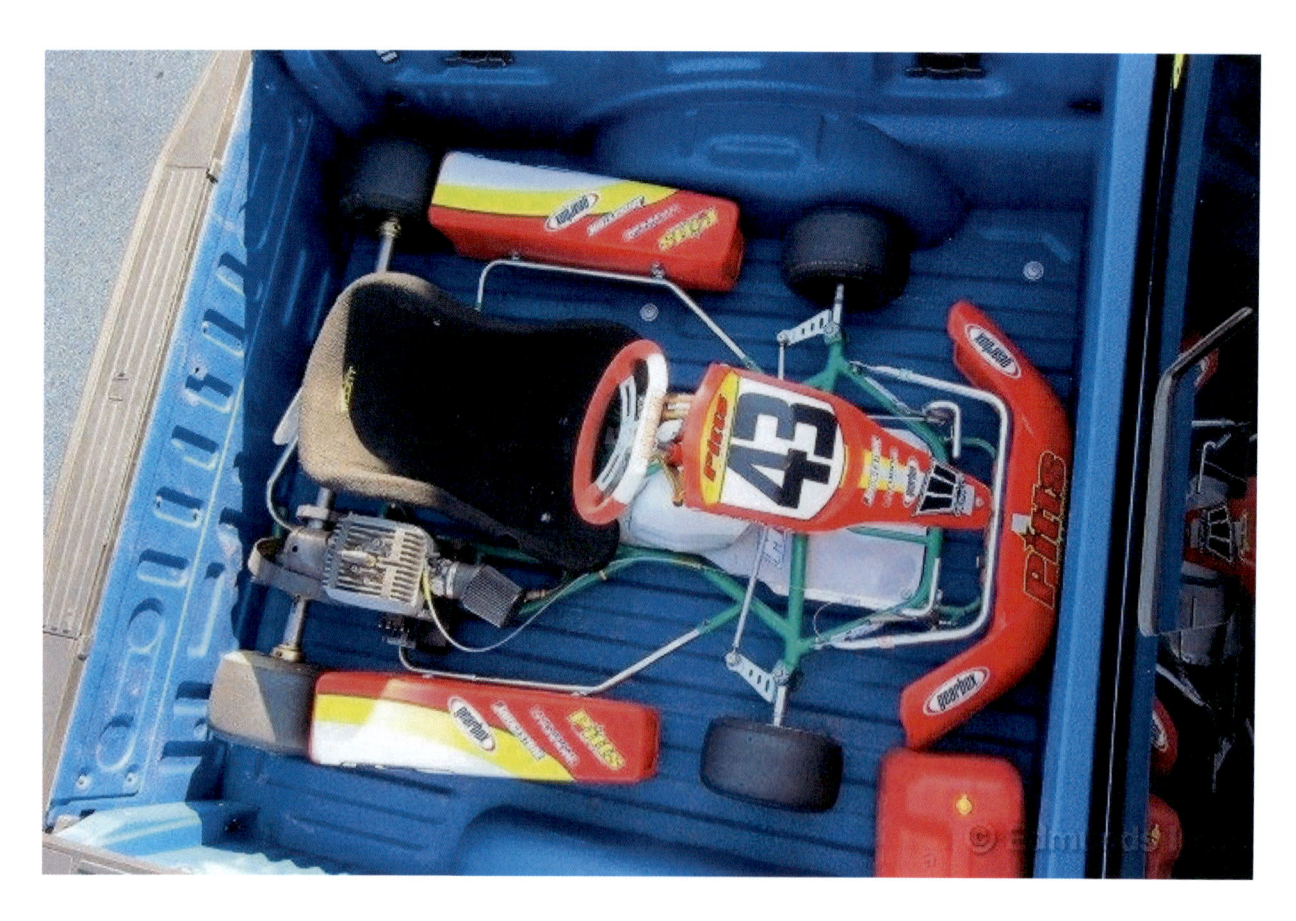

While a trailer may not always be in your budget, a small pickup or moderate size SUV will also do quite well. Here, a kart fits in the bed of a small truck with little to no disassembly. (PC: Fast100karting.com)

In most cases, a pickup truck with a normal sized bed will fit most karts with relative ease. In the case of a short bed pickup, the kart may fit by lowering the tailgate, allowing the rear tires to sit upon it as you move down the road. In the case of the open pickup, a kart cover is always a good investment, to prevent excessive rain or dust from getting on your kart. Most karts can easily be secured by 1 or 2 ratchet style straps. **It is highly recommended to secure your kart or other heavy objects in a truck, trailer, or other vehicle by a ratcheting-type tie-down strap only.** 'Cinch' type, tension, and bungees straps are prone to loosen or break when transporting a kart or other objects.

While your exact method of getting a kart to and from the track is open to interpretation, don't let ownership of a small car or something other than a large trailer discourage you! If you are truly stuck with transportation options, most kart racers at one point or another needed to find a creative transport solution of their own. By walking through the pits at any karting event, you will see many different solutions to the same fundamental challenge that transporting your kart can present.

84 | Karting 101: An Overview of Competitive Kart Racing

Karting is a sport that brings together people of varying occupations, financial means, and attitudes. At some point, all karters were where you are now: wondering how they can begin karting! (PC: OnTrack Promotions)

"What Now?" Taking Your First Steps into Karting

You've made it! If you have read "Karting 101" to this point, you hopefully now have a basic understanding of what karting is all about. We've given you an overview of the kart, racing series, basic tools you may need, and even how to get the kart to and from the track. Now, however, I bet you are wondering about the next steps. Where can you go to learn about karting? How much will it cost me? What are my options near me to go kart racing, or even try a go kart?

In this final section of "Karting 101," we will discuss some of the steps you may want to take to dip your toe into the world of karting. For many, a go kart can be a sizeable investment if they have not had the opportunity to experience them first. Fortunately, many in karting have worked to put in place opportunities for a complete newbie to get a taste of the performance and fun they will have once they get behind the wheel of these amazing machines.

While the exact infrastructure and programs available to you will vary considerably based upon your location across the globe, this section of "Karting 101" has outlined some of the common methods people use to get a taste for the sport. This includes visiting your local kart track, taking in a karting event, test driving a kart through a driving school or a private party, and trying out indoor karting facilities or series. In addition, some tips for how to go about looking at and purchasing your first kart, as well as a basic discussion of some rough cost estimates will be outlined.

This section is meant to offer some general suggestions for how to go about finding out about the sport of karting, and what it can mean to you. In many cases, you may want to do multiple activities to find out more information prior to purchasing your own kart getting seriously involved in the sport.

Visiting Your Local Kart Track

While most kart tracks are rather quiet in terms of activity when a racing event is not occurring, many are open to visitors during regular business hours as well as weekends. Often your local kart track is a great place to begin chatting with karters about their racing and learn about the sport. (PC: OnTrack Promotions)

For many in karting, one of the most exciting moments on any race day or time spent at a track is the rounding of the corner, crown of a hill, or exit off the highway that gives one a first glimpse of the racetrack. Kart tracks continue to be one of the best expressions of all the fun and memories kart racers experience together, whether racing or enjoying a day of practice or driving. For this reason, we have presented visiting your local kart track as one of the best ways to get an initial taste of the sport. Most performance kart tracks are located in suburban or rural areas, based outside of or within driving distance of larger urban centers.

Naturally, finding your closest track is the first priority. While many kart tracks have a presence online, a recent study by Kart Pulse found that over 25% of karts in some regions do not even have their track registered online. As a result, a quick Google search will likely return some of the kart tracks nearby, but may not show all. The tracks that will appear first in your internet search depends largely on your location, type of kart racing present in your region, or even the overall budget of these tracks. Because of these reasons, don't be overly discouraged if the first track you find is a considerable distance away. As you continue your search and research into karting, you may find other tracks in your local area that are not listed, or are closer to your home.

After you have found a track that looks interesting, reach out to the staff by telephone to confirm that the address listed on their site is correct for the track. It is not entirely uncommon for a track to have a seemingly basic street address, but for real-life navigation to the track to be slightly more complicated. Take some time to confirm their hours of business, and who you may be able to meet with when you come to the track. Most karting facilities are excited at telling new karters about the sport, and may have a particular member or members of their staff that specialize in the questions a new racer may have.

Once at the track, take some time to simply take in any on track activity present at the facility. If you plan correctly, you may visit a track for this first time during a race day or a busy practice day. Take note to look for some of the officials covered in this document, and **respect the spectator boundaries that the track has in place**. Listen to the sounds of the engines, smell the exhaust, and listen to the announcer if they are present. This is your first experience of kart racing, and it is important to note your general takeaways, as they will govern your subsequent interest and actions taken to get involved in karting.

While not always the case, many kart tracks have a 'pro shop' or permanent facilities associated with the track. These facilities would generally fall under the 'karting retailers' that we have already discussed. The staff and personnel on hand in these shops are often some of the best people to talk to initially about karting within your region.

In some circumstances, a kart track may have rental karts available for you to get your first taste of the sport. The types of karts, rates, and general upkeep of these karts can vary. **It is up to you to utilize your best common-sense judgment on whether or not these karts represent a sound financial and generally safe choice for your first experience of karting.**

While a driving school or test drive of a kart is a great way for many to get their first taste of karting, for others simply visiting a kart racing event as a spectator is a great first step. Unlike many other sports, karting is highly accessible to the general public. In many cases, a spectator can wander the paddock, observing competitors in their pits working on their kart, and talking about the day's events. The next section will offer some general comments about how to go about visiting your first kart race.

Visiting a Kart Race

A karting event provides interested members of the public with the opportunity to observe multiple karts on the track at once, and to ask real kart racers questions about their experience in karting. (PC: On Track Promotions)

For many people, visiting a kart race provides another great opportunity to see karts on the track competing against each other, and to see how your local karting series run their events. Depending on the region you are located in, there are likely multiple karting series that are holding events on multiple weekends throughout the warmer months of the year. In certain regions, karting events can be held in cooler months like January or December, but most kart racing activity will be found between the months of April and October.

Whether a local, regional, or national karting series, almost all racing series have an online presence. A series website usually outlines their schedule and provides general information about the karting classes they will host at each race event. At any karting event, multiple competitors will be in attendance. While the classes, type of karts, and number of participants can vary widely from one karting event to another, most events will feature multiple racers in each class, with varying levels of experience often present. It should be noted that if you attend a regional or national karting event, it is best to keep in mind that many of the karts and racers you see are likely to spend considerably more money and time at the track and on karting than you may wish to initially. This is not to say that a regional or national event may not represent karting in the best manner for you, but the level of competition present at these events is important to keep in mind and consider.

When you arrive at a karting event, you must remember that racing officials, competitors, and participants are first and foremost focused on their race day, kart, and doing their best to succeed at their work that day. This does *not,* however, mean that you can't approach karters at all! Often, at any point during the raceday you will find a handful of racers lounging in

88 | Karting 101: An Overview of Competitive Kart Racing

chairs near their kart, or in the stands observing other karting events. If, however, karters appear to be performing extensive work on their kart or are in animated conversation, the author recommends that you avoid approaching until these participants seem less busy.

Once you find a competitor that seems to be relaxing between events (note: not working animatedly on their kart), introduce yourself as a new karter. As a general rule, almost all karters remember when they were starting out in the sport, and will smile broadly. Due to the amount of time and effort they spend on their kart, most are more than happy to tell you about their experience in karting with a candidness and openness that is not commonly found in many sports. While it is great to speak with even just one karter at these events, if you are looking to find out more information about karting in your region, speaking with multiple people will provide you with the most holistic grouping of perspectives, budgets, and backgrounds that can help you gain the best insight into kart racing in your area.

In most cases, the race day will begin with one or more practice sessions for all classes present. In these sessions, a karter will perfect their kart's handling as well as their driving. After these sessions, a qualifying session will be held for each class. In these events, drivers often push their kart and driving abilities to the limit, working to register the fastest lap time they can. In most cases, the lap time that each driver produces in qualifying is used to set the starting lineup for the racing events of the day. Following qualifying, the fastest driver is usually awarded the 'pole' position for their pre-main events, which means that they start on the front row towards the inside of the track. Every other driver is subsequent grid position in the order in which they qualified: 2nd fastest laptime in qualifying starts second in pre main, 3rd fastest in third, etc (it should be noted that some oval track karting events will adjust a random or set number of participants from qualifying to their pre-main lineups). Once the qualifying and resultant pre-main lineup is set, most racing series will give participants at least one pre-main before the main racing event of the day. These pre-mains are a shorter version of the main event race, and many racers use these events to try a setup change, or advance their position from a sub-par qualifying performance. In most cases, the order in which drivers finish the pre-main events determines their final starting position for the main event. Ran at the end of the race day, a main event is the final test for kart racers. While the track type, number of laps, and the number of competitors present in the main event can vary from region to region and series to series, almost all karting events use the main event to determine the overall winner and placement for competitors on that race day. Once the main events are complete, a podium is usually set up, and awards are distributed to the main event winners and top finishers.

While there is no strict rule for the timing of karting events, a typical race day for a sprint kart event will begin around 7am, and end by 5pm. For oval track races, a similar schedule can be followed, but many can race at night as late as 12pm in the evening. Endurance and Laydown racing is typically held during a similar timespan as most sprint kart races.

Test Driving a Kart

Like any major investment, getting an experience of a kart can be a good idea before purchasing one for yourself. Many kart tracks provide rental karts and training for new racers to get their first taste of the sport, while also learning some of the basics about how to drive safely and have fun! (PC: Sabino DeCastro)

As we have discussed many times throughout "Karting 101," the exact opportunities available to each new or potential karter can vary significantly. In the case of test driving a kart, the opportunities available to you can be formerly structured, or may come as the result of prolonged discussions with a member of your local karting community. Regardless of how the opportunity presents itself near where you live, test driving a kart to get a sense for the performance, speed, and fun you can have in one is a great idea prior to purchasing your first kart.

Upon your initial search, you may find several different schools or options near you to try out karting. Some may be indoor kart tracks (see our indoor karting section), others may be performance or rental karts at a local kart track, and some may even be to schedule a test drive with a karter in the community that has been generous enough to provide their kart for such a purpose. Each opportunity may have its own costs, features, and benefits. Take your time to find the option that looks like the most feasible economically, but don't forget to factor in your desire to have fun, and be safe.

When evaluating test driving options, pay attention to the safety gear available, and remember that it is ultimately up to you to decide which option presents the safest and most comprehensive opportunity for you to experience karting in a safe and educational manner. Whether a formal karting school or a local racer, every kart test drive will have both on-track and off-track instructional components. This instruction can be as simple as describing the racing course, and the basics of how to operate the kart. Some schools or kart test drive programs will be significantly more involved, with detailed track walks, discussion of driving theory, and driving basics included.

Whether on the track with others or by yourself for your first time, the sense of the speed, performance, and ability of go karts are often the first things that a new driver will note. For many, the first laps in a kart are the beginning of a life-long love for the sport of karting. (PC: Carl Manley)

As you head out on to the track for the first time, focus on the basic instructions you have received. As you become more comfortable in the kart, begin to consider if the performance and driving experience of a kart is right for you. If you reach the conclusion that a kart is something you would like to race or drive more in the future, mention it to your instructors or kart owners. They will likely be able to help you find some of your first resources in your area that can be helpful in your efforts to dive deeper into the sport of karting. If, however, you decide that the physical strain, financial commitment, or even the experience of driving a kart is not for you, that's a positive result as well. You have safely and prudently sampled karting for yourself prior to investing your time and money in owning a kart yourself.

Indoor Karting

While typically slower than their performance specific counterparts, rental or indoor karts are a great place to start if you want to jump into a kart to simply get a very basic understanding of what a kart is like to drive. Keep in mind that the heavy weight, small engine, and poorly performing tires of an indoor kart usually only faintly hint at the true capability a high-performance kart can deliver in the corners. (PC: YouTube)

For many in a major urban area, it is likely that you have seen ads or even been to a local indoor karting facility already. Each and every year, an average of 50,000 people will visit each of these local karting facilities, each gaining a small glimpse at the performance a truly bespoke racing kart can deliver. In some cases, a new karter can practice some of the basics of kart driving at their local indoor kart track.

Most of these facilities are in largely industrial parts of town, and feature many amenities that you may not find at other karting facilities: Restaurants, a streamlined registration process, and some classroom instruction on safely driving the karts. Most have a track map, and the prices for most of these venues are within a budget for even the most cost-conscious karter. With growing frequency, it is common for members of the performance karting community to recommend that people try out indoor karting prior to purchasing a kart for themselves. While this may not be the best option for all new karters, it is one that many choose.

Once you have familiarized yourself with the track and the kart, begin analyzing the performance that these karts can deliver. Although distant cousins of true performance karting machines, many indoor karts can still achieve speeds in excess of 40 mph, and will perform in much the same way in the tighter corners. As you turn the wheel into the corner, you may feel the kart flex and rotate around the corner with much greater agility than your street car or truck. The rate at which indoor karts accelerate and decelerate is muted when compared to a shifter kart, but is substantial compared to many other vehicles. In some cases, your friends or other competitors can also give you your first taste at wheel-to-wheel racing, which is often the most engaging part for many fans of indoor karting.

Indoor karting facilities often feature leagues or competition events that cater to several levels of driving experience. Sprint, endurance, and team events are all options available at many indoor tracks (PC: Crains Cleveland)

Many indoor karting facilities also offer a chance to experience wheel-to-wheel racing with other visitors. Unlike most performance karts, the full-containment bumpers of indoor karts coupled with their slow speed allows for many to experience what it is like to race wheel to wheel with other drivers, with inevitable contact and some spins made less costly for all involved by the low speeds involved. These indoor karting facilities can also offer racing leagues, some even featuring experience or professional instruction from kart racers or other racing drivers.

Guidelines for Purchasing Your First Go Kart

Purchasing your first kart is one of the most exciting and challenging activities for many that are new to karting. Factors to consider when purchasing that first kart include your budget, desired performance, and local support options. Take your time when considering your first karting purchase. (PC: On Track Promotions)

For many, the time to consider purchasing their first kart comes after some initial research, a test drive in another person's kart, and after considering the available karting options near them. Like any major investment, there is no one-size-fits-all way to go about looking at, purchasing, or considering what option makes the best first kart for you. However, many factors that can often contribute to your ultimate buying decision include your budget, aspirations, and of course the karts available for sale locally.

As is the case for many decisions surrounding karting, the factors at play when considering the purchase of a kart are numerous. However, one of the biggest factors to consider when thinking about getting into karting is the type of kart racing that is common in your geographic region. After all, it is likely not a great idea to purchase an oval track kart if most events and tracks in your area cater to sprint karts. In most cases, the local karting infrastructure found near you will likely cater to the type of kart racing that is most popular in your geographic region. .

Another factor to consider when investigating buying a kart is your initial aspirations regarding competition. As a new karter, you may not have the best answer for this just yet. With this in mind, unless you have extensive prior racing experience, it is a generally agreed-upon

94 | Karting 101: An Overview of Competitive Kart Racing

recommendation amongst karters that a new driver should consider a kart and performance level that is best in line with your experience. That is to say, it is better to begin racing a kart that has an approachable amount of performance. While many choose to ignore this advice and purchase the most powerful shifter kart right away, these drivers tend to form poor driving habits, become frustrated with the extensive maintenance required, and are constantly intimidated by the disparity that exists between their own driving abilities and the true performance limits of the kart. It is important for a new karter to remember that a Just like a new motorcycle rider should think twice before buying the latest and greatest sport bike, so too should a new karter think long and hard before buying the fastest, shiniest kart they can get their hands on.

Like any major buying decision, another factor to consider is your realistic budget. While a brand new kart may offer the latest performance features and seem like the best choice, it is important to realize that many used karts for sale today are likely capable of giving a new driver the same satisfaction and thrill that a brand new kart would at a fraction of the costs. In the next section, some (very) rough estimates of prices for many karting items will be outlined. Extensive research and careful thought regarding your feasible buying options should be conducted prior to buying your first kart, new or used.

Lastly, a new or used kart is subject to factors largely out of the seller's control. Namely, a specific chassis or piece of karting equipment may not hold the same value within different regions. This is governed by the local karting infrastructure surrounding your regional karting community. A particular type of kart racing, a set of engine packages, and even certain brands are likely to be more valuable to a new karter than others. While unfair in many cases to the seller, the reality is that karting equipment requires regular maintenance and repair. And, while as we have stated before it is often within the ability of the kart's owner, sometimes a particular part or service requires a local karting facility or retailer to assist in the form of repair service or parts.

Logically, this region-specific specialization means that a kart that aligns with the parts and brands that local retailers service and can provide assistance with are a much smarter investment for many new karters. Many local karting retailers are specialize in a handful of chassis brands, aftermarket parts, and engine packages. The result of this is that you will notice a particular set of chassis brands, engine packages, and karting choices made within your local karting community. While several national and international karting retailers offer great support, obtaining the right part for a dated or obscure chassis is often a nightmare that new karters do not wish to experience. Suddenly, that bargain kart has become a significant challenge to keep in running order.

When considering the purchase of a kart, all the factors above should be considered extensively. Once you have determined the type of racing, budget, and major brands that are popular in your region, it is time to consider whether to invest in a new kart, or to purchase used equipment. As mentioned previously, a used kart is often a great place for most new karters to begin their karting experience. However, in some cases it can be advantageous to consider a new kart as a viable option.

For many new racers, purchasing a used kart can be a great way to enter the sport at a lower price point while still obtaining a racing machine that is likely to challenge your driving abilities for several seasons. However, a used kart should be viewed with caution. Checking for signs of excessive wear to the chassis, engine, and damage to the kart is always a prudent idea. In the case of this used kart, the kart appears to be in good condition at first glance. However, Rotax-powered karts are not typically equipped with front brakes, which could make the price of this kart abnormally high when you consider the engine package that comes with it. (PC: Shminhe)

When considering purchasing a new kart, take your time to consider all the options available to you. In many cases, several makes of chassis, engine types, and resultant overall costs will be presented to you. Don't be afraid to question a sales representative as to why a certain kart is better or worse, and make sure that you are intentional about the level of karting you want to begin with. Just like any sport, it is very easy to become entranced with the shiniest and brightest piece of kit on the sales floor. But, before you write the check or swipe your card on a brand new kart, ask yourself the following questions: "Do I really need a ceramic brake rotor rather than a steel one? For my first kart, should I be considering a 125cc engine, or a more reasonable displacement like a moderate 4-stroke? Should I spend my entire budget on the fastest and newest kart, or should I invest in slightly more expensive safety equipment?" While the ultimate answer to these questions varies from person to person, many may put away their checkbook or card, and reconsider another option: buying a used kart.

For many new racers, a great place to start when purchasing their first kart is a used kart. Like a new kart, factors to consider when purchasing a used kart should include the make of the chassis, the general upkeep evident on the kart, and of course the engine package associated with it. While not all used karts have an engine associated with the kart, it is much more common for an engine package to be offered for sale with a used kart when compared to a new kart. Like many things in motorsport, a kart depreciates significantly in value the moment it hits the track for the first time. However, a low-time used kart can still be priced fairly to 70-80% of the original sale price, depending on the general state of the kart once it is put up for sale.

By viewing several karts in various states of care and use can begin to give you a good gauge for when a used karting package is overpriced, or when the asking price is fair. Some other things to always look for with a used kart is the general state of the underside of the kart. If the kart has had many off-track excursions, one area that of the kart that most sellers neglect to alter is the underside. Excessive scraping, tearing, or lacerations to the paintwork on the chassis on the underside of the chassis can be a sign of a well-worn, or even bent chassis. Obviously, a kart that shows excessive signs of wear in this area is cause for concern. Other factors to consider when looking at a used kart includes the history of the run-time and maintenance put on the engine, the general use and driving hours put on the chassis, and of course, the price point compared to a new chassis or kart.

In some cases, a 'race used' chassis is a choice that provides a compromise between a brand new kart and a truly used kart. While a premier racing team may not be near you, many major chassis importers keep 'race used' karts in their inventory to sell to the ambitious new karter. These kart chassis and engines are typically raced at first by a national-level competitor. However, after a handful of races under a 'factory tent,' the distributor will inspect and clean these karts, and put them up for sale for the general public. By purchasing a race used chassis, a new karter can obtain a chassis that is essentially brand new with a price tag that is significantly below brand new pricing. As with any used kart, race used karts should be approached with a measured and careful assessment.

Conclusion

I want to thank you for taking the time to read about the sport of karting. Your initial impulse of interest in the sport was the catalyst for the creation of "Karting 101." Whether this document has succeeded in increasing your interest in the sport or not, without you, there is no karting. After all, if it weren't for curious passers-by in Pasadena, Art Ingels and Lou Bourelli would have long ago given up on their 'go-kart,' yet another idea by creative craftsmen reduced to the trash pile. Like those curious first few spectators, you have realized perhaps only subconsciously that driving can be more than a boring act of repetitive 'A to B' days. Every go kart raced worldwide is a symbol of the belief that driving can be perfected, considered, and explored beyond your normal commute. This belief is shared by motorsports enthusiasts across the world.

"Karting 101" was created to serve as an educational resource for the general public in regards to the sport of competitive kart racing. After reading "Karting 101," it is my hope that you have gained a greater understanding of a sport that has challenged and engaged thousands of people across the world for the last six decades. After reading every page of this document, you likely will still have unanswered questions. If you do, then I have succeeded in keeping you engaged in learning more about the sport!

For some, karting represents a continual spectrum of motorsports-related challenges that will fill their spare time, weekends, and daydreams for a significant portion of their life. Some may also enter the sport with the concrete goal of learning the fundamental skills necessary to excel at any form of motorsport. For most, however, karting will teach them about much more than driving lines and passing strategies. As I reflect upon my time in karting, it was often the lessons I learned outside of the kart that permeated other facets of my life most profoundly.

After reading "Karting 101", it is my hope that you may now consider yourself a member of the karting community. As you begin to chat with other karters at your local racetrack, or take your first laps in a kart, it is important to remember that karting is a sport that will continue to challenge you for years to come. While at times the challenges may seem insurmountable for a multitude of reasons, karting tends to reward those that work for their goals, and take the time to prepare to achieve them. If a certain lap time, karting class, or budget goal is not within your reach on your first day in karting, it is important to remember that the local club champion did not become a skilled kart racer overnight.

I want to personally thank you for taking time to read "Karting 101." Distilling the sport of karting into 100 pages has been a challenge, but one that I have sincerely enjoyed.

Above all else, remember to **have fun** in karting, and be safe!

--Eric Gunderson

About the Author: Eric Gunderson

Eric Gunderson was introduced to the world of motorsports in 2004. Within a few months of visiting a local kart racing school, Eric and his family were traveling to karting events across the Southwest. While karting was initially a family hobby, by 2007 Eric was a regional and grand national-champion in sprint kart racing. In 2008, the young driver from San Diego, California entered the oval-track racing ladder system, progressing upward through several disciplines of racecars with consistent success. While the tracks, competitors, and vehicles changed over the years, Eric's belief in the value of karting never wavered.

In 2012, Eric stepped away from racing temporarily to attend the University of Colorado, where he received a Bachelor's in Geology, and a minor in business. Upon completing his education, Eric re-entered the sport of karting in 2016, serving as an official with The Colorado Karting Tour. He also founded Apex Predator Driver Development, which teaches kart racers of all ages how to improve their driving abilities.

"Karting 101" was the result of the time that Eric spent at The Colorado Karting Tour. As he began to integrate into the local karting community, he realized that there was a stark disparity between his knowledge of karting, and the information available to the general public about the sport he loved and actively engaged in. With the support and encouragement of his colleagues at CKT, Eric began to draft the initial sections that are now present in this document.

Acknowledgements

Among the many lessons the sport of karting taught me, one that I try to reflect upon every day is that no man is an island. Like any other major project I have undertaken, "Karting 101" was the result of my initial writing, and a lot of comments, advice, and critique from my friends, fellow karters, and, eventually, the general public. While there were many people that I want to thank for their help, there have been a few exceptional partners that have provided detailed advice and content that enhanced the final product you see before you today.

On Track Promotions was one of the first to bring their support and quality images to this publication. Without exaggeration, I can say that I have been a long-time admirer of the work that OTP does. Their outstanding presentation, quality, and professionalism throughout this entire project has been humbling and greatly appreciated. Without their blessing, many of the photos I wished to use in this work to further explain a concept or piece of gear would not have been possible.

Comet Kart Sales is known across the country as one of the largest online karting-specific retailers. As a karter, I have spent a considerable amount of time on the phone speaking with their experienced representatives, and have personally benefitted from their advice and inventory in my own racing. At the beginning of this project, it was to their own "Karting 101" that I first turned. Many of the sections and comments I have illustrated in great detail in this publication were the result of receiving Comet Kart Sale's agreement to utilize their work as a source of inspiration in this project.

Lastly, but certainly not least, I have to mention my friends and colleagues at The Colorado Karting Tour. Without my time served as an official with this racing series, it is unlikely that I would be in a position to even consider writing "Karting 101." It was, after all, in one of many conversations with the president of the club, Scott Williams, that the idea for "Karting 101" was first developed. As I began to write, it became clear that this document could serve the greater karting community, not just CKT. The dedication, local karting focus, and sportsmanship I have seen as an official with CKT has been extremely humbling, and gave me many experiences that were useful when writing this content for the true beginner in the sport of karting.

In addition to these major supporters, the karting community has been more than generous with their advice, critique, and suggestions.